Making Better Law

Reform of the legislative process from policy to Act

D0416590

HANSARD
SOCIETY

Ruth Fox & Matt Korris

About the authors

Ruth Fox – Director of the Hansard Society's Parliament and Government Programme.

Matt Korris – Research Fellow on the Hansard Society's Parliament and Government Programme.

The **Parliament and Government Programme** undertakes research to stimulate reform of political institutions and the parliamentary process with a particular focus on the Westminster Parliament. Our research is at the forefront of debate about the role of Parliament and parliamentarians, the future of representative democracy, and the public's engagement with politics and the political process.

We are happy to invite analysis and discussion of the views put forward in this report. For more information contact the Parliament and Government Programme at: parliamentprogrammeathansard@hansard.lse.ac.uk

Acknowledgements

This report could not have been produced without the on-going assistance of Fiona Booth, Virginia Gibbons, Kate Egglestone and Diana Stirbu.

The Making Better Law project was the original brainchild of Alex Brazier and we have been grateful for his continuing advice and commitment to it. Peter Riddell and Daniel Greenberg have also provided invaluable comments at various stages.

We would particularly like to thank Laura Thornton, Geetha Mazarelo and Kristina Wollter for their research support as well as Nicola Atkins, Juliana Bruton, Amy Drake, James Easy, Clare Huxley, Josh Niderost, Katie Russell, Andrew Scott-Taggart and Sherri Whitehead for help with the seminars and the research. Our thanks also to Mona Petre for the front cover design.

This study would not have been possible without the involvement of all those who took part in the Making Better Law seminars. They are too numerous to mention here but are listed in the Appendix. We have greatly appreciated all their contributions, but particularly those who presented papers and took part in the panels at the seminars, namely: Professor the Lord Norton of Louth, Chris Huhne MP, Professor Stefan Vogenauer, Lord Bichard, Professor Philip Cowley, Stephen Laws CB, Professor Jeremy Horder, Baroness Hamwee, Robert Rogers, Sir Richard Tilt, and Michael Clancy.

Above all our thanks go to the Nuffield Foundation for supporting this project from the outset, particularly Anthony Tomei, Sharon Witherspoon, and Baroness O'Neill of Bengarve.

Contents

Preface

Improving the way legislation is prepared and taken through Parliament has been a central focus of the Hansard Society's research and publications for more than two decades.

The thorough and authoritative report of the Rippon Commission in 1993 highlighted many of the themes which have been taken up regularly since then in a series of reports: the dangers of ill-prepared and hastily drafted bills; of inadequate and partial scrutiny by Parliament (particularly the House of Commons); and of enabling bills which leave key decisions to later secondary legislation. The remedies have been easier to state than achieve: clearer, simpler bills; more consultation both before and after publication; more scope for parliamentary scrutiny and amendment; and, above all, less legislation.

There have been improvements, but the record has been mixed. More bills are published in draft form, but not nearly enough and seldom the most controversial ones. More bills are subject to pre-legislative scrutiny (and some now to post-legislative examination after enactment), but there is often insufficient time. A shift away from the previous imposition of guillotines to formal timetables at the start of a bill's progress in the Commons has provided more predictability but many key clauses are still often left unexamined by MPs.

This latest report is based on a series of seminars held in 2009 with a wide range of political, official, professional and academic practitioners, three of which I chaired. The emphasis was on the practical: reviewing the current position and looking at workable solutions.

The new Parliament has started with many grand sounding phrases about a 'new politics' and a 'fresh spirit of reform'. But the record has been less positive: several major bills, including constitutional measures, have been introduced with scarcely any time for adequate consultation or scrutiny. This report underlines how much there is still to do.

Rt Hon Peter Riddell
Chair
Hansard Society

Executive summary

- The executive has a right to implement its legislative programme but Parliament has an obligation to ensure that the laws that are passed are of the highest possible quality, having been subject to appropriate levels of consultation, preparation and scrutiny.

- Government and Parliament should recognise that they do not have a monopoly on expertise, particularly in highly technical fields of law, and the scrutiny of such legislation would therefore benefit from external support.

- Procedural tools that would demonstrably help improve the quality of legislation are already in existence but they are not sufficiently embedded in the day-to-day work of government and Parliament.

- If the quality of law-making is to be improved there needs to be a significant cultural and attitudinal shift in thinking in both Whitehall and Westminster.

- Improving legislation is a goal that will not be accomplished cheaply.

- Parliament and government should not be afraid to test, innovate, evaluate, learn and revise to build on the piecemeal reforms and practices of the past.

- A new Parliament offers an early window of opportunity for reform – the governing parties are on record as recognising the problems with deficient legislation and say they are committed to resolving them; a new generation of MPs have the opportunity to make their mark as reformers.

Chapter 1: Bad law: a diagnosis

- There is no single cause of deficient legislation. The explanation lies in a complex confluence of factors primarily related to volume, attitude, preparation and deliberation.

- The sheer volume of legislation now being produced combined with its increasing complexity places huge pressure on the legislative process and parliamentary time and resources.

- The attitude of the executive to the legislative process contributes to and reinforces the problems. Successive governments have treated the legislative programme as a form of extended press release.

- Ministers are too often tempted to utilise their 'legislative opportunity' as a vehicle to take forward whatever policy ideas they may have at hand, resulting in 'Christmas Tree bills' on which hang a huge number of 'miscellaneous provisions' that are then difficult for parliamentarians to scrutinise.

- Regular ministerial reshuffles mean ministers have rarely been in post long enough to deal with the results of the legislation they have passed. This is reinforced by similar weaknesses in civil service corporate memory.

- Parliament and government operate to different timetables – government requires quick decisions; Parliament requires time for deliberation – the rhythm of their work is thus in conflict.

- The legislative process should be streamlined by government and Parliament to maximise strengths, avoid duplicative work and make best use of resources.

- The late addition of substantive government amendments to bills in progress and the increased use of delegated legislation are major obstacles to good scrutiny and lead to legislation that is constitutionally and procedurally deficient.

Chapter 2: Moving from policy to law: the role of external expertise

- The volume and increasingly complex technical nature of legislation heightens the need for effective and early engagement and consultation with external policy experts.

- Consultations on legislation should be more structured, and focus much more clearly on choices and priorities, taking respondents through competing arguments and the consequences of each choice.

- Use of the *Code of practice on consultation* should be more effectively monitored and enforced.

- There should be more detailed consultation feedback presented to Parliament and the public following consideration of bills (in draft or full form).

- Civil servants should take a more pro-active approach to the commissioning of research, identifying and promoting to academics those priority areas where research would most aid their strategic policy development work.

- Support for the development of 'co-production' models for research, knowledge brokers and policy entrepreneurs, should be explored and policy-makers should consider greater piloting of proposals wherever possible in order to provide insight and a clear evidence base for legislative changes.

- An example of good practice for improving evidence-based analysis of legislative proposals – the Social Security Advisory Committee (SSAC) – should be replicated in other technically complex areas of policy.

Chapter 3: Drafting, access to and quality of the statute book

- The drafting process is a significant determining factor in the quality of the resulting bill. That legislation should be accessible, intelligible and clear to all audiences is both a democratic right and also an essential prerequisite in the process of making better law.

- A Legislative Draft Readers' Panel should be established on a trial basis in this Parliament to provide some light-touch external oversight of the work of the Office of the Parliamentary Counsel (OPC).

- The OPC should agree a protocol with government departments to ensure technical issues are included in all future draft bill consultation documents.

- An online crowd-source public drafting project should be piloted for one bill in this Parliament.

- Keeling-like Schedules should become a standard element of explanatory notes to a bill, and be updated as the bill progresses through each stage of legislative scrutiny as required.

- The government should pilot some of the plain language drafting support models utilised overseas and continue to trial the use of plain English bills.

- Parliament should trial the use of mobile, hand-held technology (e.g. PDAs and tablet computers) in the Chamber.

- Consideration should be given to requiring government departments to bring forward consolidation measures on a fixed basis or to report on the options for consolidation within their legislative remit on a regular timescale.

Chapter 4: Reform and innovation in legislative scrutiny

Legislative standards
- Parliament should establish a Legislative Standards Committee, ideally on a bi-cameral basis, to assess the necessity of legislation and whether the technical quality of a bill has met an agreed minimum set of standards and criteria.

- A new Legislative Impact Assessment should be required in order to provide members with more detailed information about a bill.

Timing
- There is scope for much greater use of the sessional carry-over procedure.

- The Procedure Committee should explore the merits of moving consideration of bills to a legislative rather than a sessional cycle.

- A review of the operation of programming should be undertaken with a view to rebalancing the timetabling of business in favour of Parliament and improved time for scrutiny.

- A Business Committee should be established as promised within three years. Some form of Joint Business Liaison mechanism should also be established to enable cross-Chamber discussions to take place regarding how each House is to examine legislation.

House of Commons procedures
- Pre-legislative scrutiny by parliamentary committee ought to be the norm for most bills. Where possible, MPs who take part in pre-legislative scrutiny should also subsequently become members of the public bill committee.

- All bills that are subject to carry-over from one parliamentary session to another should have had pre-legislative scrutiny in draft form.

- Split committals of bills should be used more regularly, scrutinising contentious clauses in the Chamber of the House of Commons and the remainder of the bill in Public Bill Committee (PBC).

- PBC procedures should be reformed:
    - programme motions should be delayed to allow for a better assessment of the needs of the PBC to be made on the basis of the second reading debate;
    - an 'injury time' provision would allow extra time at the end of a PBC to return to clauses where debate was cut short;
    - during sittings where multiple witnesses are scheduled, it should be left to the discretion of the chair to manage time;
    - given the complexity of legislation, experts, lawyers and even officials should be permitted to speak;
    - more time is required between the evidence-gathering phase of a PBC and the line-by-line consideration of the bill.

- The House of Commons should trial the introduction of Legislative Committees to combine the membership and expertise of a select committee and PBC.

- If government tables a significant number of amendments at report stage that substantially alter the nature of a bill, a future Business Committee should be able to return it to committee stage. Where a bill has been heavily amended a full third reading should take place. When the government tables amendments to its own bill it should have to explain the reasons for doing so.

- All Acts eligible for post-legislative review between three and five years after enactment should be considered by a departmental select committee or a new Joint Committee for Post-Legislative Review.

House of Lords procedures

- The House of Lords should adopt a public evidence hearing committee for all bills that originate in the Upper House.

- Grand Committee should be the default mechanism for consideration of all bills in the Lords unless otherwise required by the House. Members of the temporary select committee that hear the public evidence session should also consider the bill at Grand Committee stage.

- When a bill passes from the Commons to the Lords any clauses that have not been debated should be 'flagged' on the order paper or the bill.

- Detailed proposals for how a reformed House of Lords will deal with legislation should be a paramount concern and priority.

Delegated legislation

- Reform of the scrutiny processes for delegated legislation is an urgent priority.

- Consideration should be given to the value of extra-parliamentary scrutiny through the establishment of a small number of independent bodies, similar in form to the Social Security Advisory Committee (SSAC).

- Agreement should be sought on the criteria to be used for deciding the specific form of Statutory Instruments (SIs) being utilised in any bill.

- The House of Commons should establish its own sifting committee for delegated legislation.

- 'Praying time' for SIs should be extended from 40 to 60 sitting days and those to be approved through the affirmative resolution procedure should be amendable.

Public engagement with the legislative process

- The trial of a new petitions and ePetitions system through a new Petitions Committee should be implemented as soon as possible.

A concordat between Parliament and government

- A comprehensive review of the legislative powers of the executive and Parliament should be undertaken with a view to drawing up a concordat that clearly sets out where key powers lie, and clarifies the relationships between and responsibilities of the executive, the legislatures and the courts.

Introduction

Laws are the essential threads that bind together our society. They provide the framework of democratically inspired and enforced rules that define us as a nation and mediate relations between each of us as citizens. Though we may not be readily conscious of it, a wide variety of laws impinge on our public and private lives each and every day. They control and shape every area of national life, from the economy to education, health, housing, the environment, immigration, public order and national security.

And yet, despite their fundamental importance to us all, the process by which we make laws in this country is deeply flawed. Whether the audience is parliamentarians who make the law, judges who have to apply it, or the public who must comply with it, it is not difficult to find vocal critics of the current system.

Many are concerned by the sheer volume of new legislation, questioning whether much of it is really justified as an ever-expanding statute book is distorted by an increasing amount of duplicative legal remedies and the introduction of new offences that are never used, or indeed never intended for use. The way that successive governments have legislated in order to meet explicitly political rather than legal imperatives, with ministers treating the legislative programme as a form of extended press release, has also become an increasing source of complaint. In these circumstances the quality of the statute they are producing is not always uppermost in ministerial minds; their primary objective is to get the law through to Royal Assent to demonstrate that the government has done *something*.

Additionally, there is widespread criticism that the quality of policy preparation and public consultation by departments – particularly the involvement of experts with specialist knowledge that could usefully be deployed in the policy development process – is inadequate and weak. Consequently the flaws and incoherence that may exist with a policy and how government proposes to implement it are not dealt with from the outset. The knock-on effects are then felt at the drafting stage when political and policy intentions take legislative shape. Accurately or not, the perception exists that all too often policy, and the laws that emerge from such policy, are dreamt up on the hoof, often in response to the pressure of the 24/7 media cycle, with insufficient thought given to the detail and consequences of the changes proposed.

Increasing pressure on parliamentary scrutiny

The bills then arrive in Parliament where MPs and peers are constitutionally responsible for putting the government's legislative ambitions under the microscope. But the torrent of legislation parliamentarians face each session and the increasingly complex and technical nature of many statutes today means that there is currently a serious mismatch between the scrutiny mission of Parliament and its capacity to carry out that mission. The pressures on scrutiny have grown as a result of the way in which we now make laws, but the resources and expertise in Parliament for this task have not grown in tandem: the scrutiny system is consequently not fit for purpose. Despite some welcome improvements in the parliamentary process in recent years, for example the advent of pre-legislative scrutiny and the replacement of the widely criticised Standing Committees with Public Bill Committees, the task of reform is not yet complete. Such are the flaws in the legislative process that further fundamental changes to the way legislation is prepared, presented to Parliament and scrutinised, are needed.

These criticisms are not new: many of these same concerns were levelled at the process almost 20 years ago when the Hansard Society's Commission on the Legislative Process (the Rippon Commission) reported deep anxiety and unhappiness with 'the way legislation is prepared, drafted, passed through Parliament and published'.[1] In 1993 the Commission published its report, *Making the Law,* which laid out a raft of recommended reforms to improve the process of legislative consultation, drafting and parliamentary scrutiny. Some of these reforms have been implemented but many remained untouched.

In the intervening years the Hansard Society has maintained its long-standing and close interest in how laws are made and how legislative procedures can be improved. This report, generously funded by the Nuffield Foundation, takes a fresh look at our system of law-making in light of recent political, economic, social and procedural changes and asks again the crucial question: can we not do it better?

In particular, this study builds upon our publication, *Law in the Making: Influence and Change in the Legislative Process*, which was published in

---

[1] Hansard Society (1993), *Making the Law: The Report of the Hansard Society Commission on the Legislative Process* (London: Hansard Society), p.1.

2008 and was also funded by the Nuffield Foundation. [2] That publication looked specifically at the impact that Parliament has on legislative proposals and the changes and improvements it is able to make to bills as they progress through Parliament to Royal Assent. The focus of that study was on the parliamentary scrutiny process. This new study broadens the scope to look at how government converts policy into legislative form, how consultation and external expertise are brought into the process, and how wider political pressures affect law-making. Our conclusion is that the system is found wanting in many respects.

'Making Better Law' seminars

In 2009 the Hansard Society hosted four seminars under Chatham House rules to explore these issues with an eclectic body of experts drawn from Parliament (members and officials), academia, the civil service, the legal profession and civil society groups. [3] Papers were presented at each seminar to inform the discussion and debate around four key themes:

i.   diagnosing the causes and consequences of deficient law;

ii.   the role of external expertise in the development of policy and its shaping into legislation;

iii.   the strengths and weaknesses of the technical process of drafting laws; and

iv.   innovations in legislative scrutiny.

The organisation of this report broadly mirrors the structure of these seminars. In considering how we might make better law, our interest is not in the policy aspects of the statute book: we are not concerned here with the policy relevance and policy outcomes of legislative proposals. Perspectives on the policy aspects of legislation are necessarily subjective and largely depend on political views and preferences. Whether or not Acts of

---

[2] A. Brazier, S. Kalitowski & G. Rosenblatt with M. Korris (2008), *Law in the Making: Influence and Change in the Legislative Process* (London: Hansard Society).

[3] See Appendix I for details of the seminar participants. Throughout the report, the comments of individual participants have been attributed directly only in those instances where they were a member of the 'discussants panel' at one of the seminars. Otherwise, comments from participants have been included on a non-attributable basis.

Parliament meet the stated objectives that government sets for them is beyond the scope of this study. Our interest is in the quality of the process and procedure by which law is made, encompassing the stages of departmental consultation on policy, preparation and drafting of a bill, and parliamentary scrutiny of that legislation.

It is our contention that whilst policy is subject to the partisan political battle, the process by which legislation is considered can make a considerable difference in improving the quality of the final statute that emerges, regardless of political differences. The policy product is important but how the legislative process affects that product is our primary interest, for there are ways in which it is possible to influence the legislative process, particularly in technically complex policy areas, in order to improve it before political dynamics and the imperatives of partisan battle come into play. The chapters that follow explore how this might be achieved, particularly focusing on how external expertise and improved mechanisms for expert scrutiny might contribute to this goal.

Chapter 1, 'Bad law: a diagnosis', explores the nature of and reasons for deficient legislation including the detrimental impact of the quantity of legislation being produced by government, the political pressures which shape, often unhelpfully, the attitude of politicians and civil servants to law-making, and the damaging impact these factors can consequently have on the preparation of bills by Parliamentary Counsel and the deliberation on the legislative proposals by MPs and peers.

Chapter 2, 'Moving from policy to law: the role of external expertise', explores why improved specialist and expert input into the policy development process might enhance the legislation that emerges; why the different approach that policy-makers and researchers take to 'opinion' and 'evidence' is hindering greater involvement by experts; and in light of these problems how the consultation process might be reformed to better encourage and utilise expert advice and what other mechanisms might facilitate that greater external input into the legislative process.

Chapter 3, 'Drafting, access to and quality of the statute book', explores the technical process of legislative drafting and the role of Parliamentary Counsel, outlining the strengths and weaknesses of the current drafting system. It analyses how consultation and specialist knowledge and advice from policy and legal experts, particularly in highly complex, technical areas of law, might contribute to and enhance the process; and details how improvements might be made to enhance the clarity and integrity of the statute book, as well as public access to it.

Finally, **chapter 4, 'Reform and innovation in legislative scrutiny'**, looks at the mechanisms for parliamentary and external scrutiny of legislation that ultimately shape the quality of laws passed. It explores the structural, procedural and cultural issues that influence the effectiveness of the scrutiny process and suggests examples of reform and innovation that might provide models for improving scrutiny in the future, such as those used in the devolved legislatures.

A number of key themes emerged at these seminars and through our wider research and are explored in detail in the chapters that follow. How we currently make law is detrimentally affected by the sheer volume of legislation and by how this interacts with the challenges posed by the time that is made available for legislative preparation and deliberative scrutiny.

The cultural and attitudinal differences between Parliament and government also exercise a significant and often detrimental influence on the process. The pace of the legislature is not the same pace as that of the executive: the legislative process, with its focus on detailed scrutiny and careful deliberation operates to a different rhythm to that demanded in government. And in Parliament the legislative process itself is based on an uneasy compromise between partisan battle and dispassionate scrutiny. The adversarial system and ethos still dominates even as mechanisms for less partisan scrutiny have been introduced: the cultural change required has not yet materialised. If better law is to be made in the future then cultural and attitudinal change is needed equally as much, if not more than, procedural reform.

A strong theme of this study is that in many instances Parliament already has a range of procedural tools at its disposal that ought to make a real difference in improving legislation. However, in too many instances these tools are not being used to their fullest effect and have not been routinely embedded as a feature of the legislative process. Allowing for the fact that the work of government and Parliament is necessarily carried out at a different speed, the ultimate goal should be to streamline as far as possible the process and procedures by which law is made – in both Whitehall and Westminster – in order to secure improvements in both its efficiency and effectiveness.

Unless and until there is a change – both attitudinally and procedurally – then Parliament will continue to pay a high price in terms of reputational damage.

Parliament is judged, to a significant degree, by the quality of law it produces. Parliamentarians at Westminster must therefore give serious consideration to how long they will continue to do the 'heavy lifting' to improve legislation given the inadequate tools and resources currently at their disposal. As Sir George Young MP said in a lecture to the Hansard Society in March 2010, it is absurd to expect Parliament 'to take the hit for inadequate preparation in Whitehall'.[4] It needs to more strongly assert itself in relation to the executive in order to renew its relevance and legitimacy in the law-making process.

At its heart then, this study is a reassessment of how the relationship between Parliament and government operates through the legislative process and, in the public interest, it is an urgent call for a rebalancing of that relationship in order to ensure the making of better law in the future.

The opportunities of the 'new politics'

Since we began our research there has been a general election and the consequent emergence of a coalition government whose approach to law-making may necessarily have to be more circumspect and prescribed than its predecessor as it seeks to carry the support of members of two parties with often divergent philosophies, ambitions and commitments. The pace of government decision-making, action and legislation may therefore change naturally although the initiation of legislation such as the Academies Bill, the Public Bodies Bill and the Parliamentary Voting System and Constituencies Bill in the first few months of the coalition does not give much cause for early optimism.

Legislation at the start of a Parliament is arguably always likely to be less well-considered; any new government wishes to move quickly to establish its programme and there will be less time for important stages such as pre-legislative scrutiny. But it is a far from desirable situation.

Members of both governing parties are on record expressing serious concerns about many of the problems associated with the legislative process that are detailed in this study. The Conservative Party's *Report of the Commission to*

---

[4] Sir George Young MP, 'Parliamentary Reform: The Conservative Perspective' lecture delivered on 18 March 2010, in Hansard Society (2010), *The Reform Challenge – Perspectives on Parliament: Past, Present and Future* (London: Hansard Society), p.52.

Strengthen Parliament in 2000 chaired by Lord Norton, and more recently the reports issued by the Democracy Taskforce chaired by Ken Clarke MP in the last Parliament, highlighted concerns about how legislation was prepared, introduced and scrutinised and suggested a range of reforms for tackling the problems.[5] Now in government, the Ministry of Justice, led by Ken Clarke, has been set the strategic objective to 'assure better law' as one of its departmental structural reform priorities over the course of this Parliament. To this end, the government plans to repeal what it deems unnecessary and duplicative laws in a new Repeal Bill to be introduced in the second session of Parliament in May 2012.[6]

It is therefore to be hoped that the coalition government will keep its assurances that its early failings will not be repeated throughout the Parliament. Every government can have the benefit of the doubt for a time at the start of its period in office; but if the government is serious about reform and is committed to addressing the deficiencies in the legislative process it cannot treat legislation in 2011 as it has in 2010.

The new government's political and constitutional reform agenda also impinges directly on debate about the law-making process: what impact will a fixed term Parliament and changes to the parliamentary sessions have, if any? Will a new Public Reading Stage for legislation make any real difference to the quality of law that emerges? Will select committees flex their muscles more when it comes to critiquing legislative proposals now that their members are elected? Will the House of Lords challenge legislation as much in the context of the new coalition politics? And, pending any long-term reform of the Upper House, if peers seek to reform their own procedures what role will addressing flawed legislation play in their prioritisation of those reforms?

The emergence of a new generation of MPs in Parliament following the biggest turnover of members since the Second World War may also have an impact. They are intent on doing, and being seen to do, things differently from their predecessors but they are understandably inexperienced and will take time to grapple with the complexities of parliamentary procedure. To what

---

[5] See for example, Professor the Lord Norton of Louth (2000), *Strengthening Parliament: The Report of the Commission to Strengthen Parliament* (London: Conservative Party); Conservative Democracy Task Force (2007), *Power to the People: Rebuilding Parliament* (London: Conservative Party).

[6] Ministry of Justice, *Business Plan 2011-2015*, November 2010, p.19.

extent, and how quickly, they will ultimately be socialised into the traditional ways of Westminster remains to be seen.[7] But certainly there is an early window of opportunity for reform if this generation are minded to make their mark on Parliament and demand changes in the way that legislation is created and scrutinised.

The answers to these questions may not be known for some years to come but the political and parliamentary environment has changed in the last year to such an extent that it is an opportune moment to re-open the debate about fundamental reform of the law-making process. But, as will become clear in the chapters that follow, structural and procedural change alone will not be sufficient to address the problems. If the quality of law-making is to be improved then there will also need to be a cultural and attitudinal shift in thinking in both Whitehall and Westminster and this may prove to be the most intractable hurdle of all. Our intention and that of the Nuffield Foundation in supporting us as we embarked on this study was to raise the profile of the subject and thereby encourage debate and analysis about these challenges. We hope that the issues we explore and the recommendations we set out will, in this new political environment, act as a catalyst for change to fundamentally improve the culture and process by which law is made in the future.

---

[7] For an examination of the socialisation of new MPs see, G. Rosenblatt (2006), *A Year in the Life: From Member of Public to Member of Parliament* (London: Hansard Society).

Chapter 1: Bad law: a diagnosis

There is no single cause of deficient legislation. The explanation lies in a complex confluence of factors primarily related to volume, attitude, preparation and deliberation.[8]

The sheer volume of legislation now being produced, combined with its increasing complexity, particularly in relation to regulatory and technical issues, places huge pressure on the legislative process and parliamentary time and resources. Our political culture prioritises executive decisiveness – exemplified by '*initiativitis*' – rather than executive reflection. It sees success in terms of the passage of legislation rather than its consequences and fosters departmental ministerial tourism (reshuffles) as a short-term quick fix to political problems with little regard for the results in terms of ministerial continuity and understanding of policy and legislation. Together, these create an environment that is not conducive to the production of high quality, well-considered law.

At its worst what often then emerges is ill-considered, ill-prepared legislation that the government then proceeds to amend, sometimes on a monumental scale. It is not unknown for the government to prepare dozens of pages of amendments to its own bill within days of it arriving in the House of Commons for consideration. Some amendments are undoubtedly the result of government 'listening' to concerns, but if 92 pages of amendments are tabled by the government to its own Constitutional Reform and Governance Bill, as occurred in February 2005, then there are strong grounds for suspecting that the legislative proposals are the product of an inadequate preparation process.

This inevitably impacts on the parliamentary scrutiny system. The government introduces its legislation followed by a programming motion to 'timetable' the bill's passage expeditiously through all its stages in the House of Commons, squeezing the time available for MPs to consult on its merits at committee stage and constraining effective scrutiny at report stage by the late tabling of amendments for consideration.

---

[8] Professor the Lord Norton of Louth, 'Bad Law: A Diagnosis', unpublished paper for the Hansard Society Making Better Law seminar, March 2009.

Collectively, the result of these pressures and problems can be a cycle of bad law. As Lord Norton concluded: 'Because Parliament cannot scrutinise the legislation to the extent necessary to prevent deficient legislation getting through, then more legislation is necessary to correct the deficiencies of the previous measures.'[9] It is his and our hypothesis that the better the parliamentary scrutiny the less likely it is that corrective legislation will be needed in the future.

This chapter explores these inter-related issues of volume, attitude, preparation and deliberation. It sets out how they impact detrimentally on the legislative process and suggests reforms to address the problems. It does so using the Home Office as a case study. It has been the most prolific legislative department over the past decade, dealing with a wide range of complex and technical issues often in the full glare of the media spotlight, and has produced legislation the quality of which has often been the subject of political and legal criticism. As such, the department's legislative record powerfully illustrates some of the causes and effects of poor law-making.

The volume of legislation

In the Westminster Parliament, government has a near-monopoly on the right to legislative initiative and as a participant observed at our first seminar, 'no government in the post-war period has been able to resist the temptation to use its powers to the limit of what the parliamentary machine is able to withstand'. As the graphs in Appendix V illustrate, the number of Public Acts produced in recent years is not out of kilter with previous decades, indeed to some extent the number of Acts has declined a little. The average number of government bills in a typical parliamentary session runs at anything between 35 and 50 depending on the length of the session, a situation that MPs in the 1940s and 1950s would have well recognised. Leo Amery, writing in 1947, was moved to remark that Parliament 'had become an overworked legislative factory' and the situation has not improved in the intervening years.[10] What is different today is that the length of Acts is significantly greater than in previous decades. Furthermore, there has been an explosion in the amount of

---

[9] *Ibid.*

[10] L.S. Amery (1964 edn), *Thoughts on the Constitution* (Oxford: Oxford University Press), p.41.

delegated or secondary legislation, both in terms of the number of Statutory Instruments (SIs) and the page length of each SI (see Appendix V). In the 1950 parliamentary session 3,690 pages of legislation – Public and General Acts and Statutory Instruments – became law; by 1970 this had grown to 5,990 and by 1990 to 8,940 pages. Just over 15 years later however, the number of pages had almost doubled to 16,031 in the 2006 session.[11] This growth in delegated legislation places extra demands on the parliamentary scrutiny process, the procedures for which are also subject to severe criticism. Crucially, primary legislation may sometimes be effectively framework legislation with much of the detail, consequences and impact of the proposals contained in the subsequent secondary legislation. This therefore constrains the ability to effectively scrutinise the primary legislation from the outset.

Explaining why this growth in legislation has taken place is complex. Certainly the role of the state has changed markedly over the decades and the extent to which it seeks to regulate the affairs of the individual and public life has had an effect on the volume and technical nature of the legislation. A significant amount of primary and secondary legislation in recent years has been regulatory measures to address and govern matters such as health and safety, animal welfare, food production standards, environmental health, and waste disposal to name just a few. The expansion of the regulatory state has particularly contributed to the increase in the volume of criminal law. As the Law Commission notes, 'Agencies to which government has granted powers to create and regulate standards of behaviour in particular areas have become much more common.'[12] It has identified over 60 national regulators with the power to make (criminal) law. As a consequence, in order to provide the support necessary for them to carry out their duties, more criminal offences have emerged, particularly through SIs.

The rapidly changing nature of technology means that the law must also change frequently in response to new advances and situations. The growth and increased complexity of the welfare state has also resulted in a massive expansion of social welfare legislation of considerable length and detail. Here,

---

[11] S. Lightbown & B. Smith, *Parliamentary Trends: Statistics About Parliament*, Research Paper 09/69, (London: House of Commons Library), August 2009, p.7.

[12] The Law Commission (2010), *Criminal Liability in Regulatory Contexts: An Overview, Consultation Paper No 195 (Overview)*, para.1.21, p.6.

there has been a developing trend against officer discretion within the benefits system as a result of which ministers seek to write every conceivable eventuality into primary or delegated legislation, considerably lengthening the bills and SIs as a consequence. Most of these trends in governance are unlikely to be significantly reversed. Therefore, the legislative and parliamentary process must adapt more fully than has previously been the case to changes in the balance of primary and secondary legislation.

Globalisation means domestic law must also respond and adapt to the emergence of new supra-national standards and international agreements. Increased legislation – particularly delegated legislation – to deal with European matters has had an impact. Assessing exactly how much of UK law is the result of European Union (EU) measures is complicated but latest estimates suggest that between 1997 and 2009, 6.8% of primary legislation and 14.1% of secondary legislation (SIs) had a role in implementing EU obligations.[13] It is suggested that the UK's declaratory system of law may also be leading to the 'goldplating' of EU measures and that legislation is being used as a cheap and quick vehicle by government to demonstrate compliance with EU directives. Firm evidence is hard to come by – and is subject to considerable political contention – but there was strong anecdotal evidence at our seminar which suggested that, as departments know the new laws will not necessarily be enforced, it is deemed a relatively cost-free mechanism compared to the expenditure of resources required to prove that existing law already covers the matter in hand. An 'encrustation of legislation' is the result. But there is of course a cost, and it is borne by Parliament in terms of the burgeoning scale and scope of legislation it must scrutinise. As one seminar participant put it, 'It is not a trivial matter to create criminal offences non-seriously.'

An increasing sense that legislation has been used to micro-manage the relationship between politicians and the judiciary has also developed over the years. Creating 'over-detailed and prescriptive legislation'[14] by increasing the number of criminal offences restricts the scope for judicial interpretation.

---

[13] V. Miller, *How much legislation comes from Europe?*, Research Paper 10/62, (London: House of Commons Library), October 2010.

[14] J.R. Spencer, 'The Drafting of Criminal Legislation: Need it be so Impenetrable?', *Cambridge Law Journal*, 67(3), November 2008, pp.585-605.

An examination of Home Office legislation alone demonstrates the scale of what Liberal Democrat MP Chris Huhne, described in his presentation at our seminar as 'legislative incontinence on a fairly massive scale'. There is some disagreement as to exactly how many pieces of criminal justice legislation have been passed since 1997, with suggestions ranging from 26 Acts up to 72, depending on the definition used.[15] In terms of purely Home Office legislation, our assessment is that between the 1997 and 2010 general elections, 47 Acts of Parliament were initiated by the Home Office, averaging about three and a half per parliamentary session.[16] Over 3,000 new criminal offences were created in this same period. Putting this in context, Law Commission analysis of the four volumes of Halsbury's Statutes of criminal law found that the offences created between the years 1351 and 1988 are contained in one volume encompassing 1,382 pages of law in total. In contrast, the 19 years between 1989 and 2008 are contained in the remaining three volumes encompassing a total of 3,746 pages of law. As the Law Commission noted, 'more than two and a half times as many pages were needed in Halsbury's Statutes to cover offences created in the 19 years between 1989 and 2008 than were needed to cover the offences created in the 637 years prior to that'.[17] The effects on the governmental and parliamentary system of such an unprecedented increase in the volume of law cannot be overestimated. Acts of Parliament passed in 2009 alone contained 2,492 new laws – an increase of 16% on 2008.[18]

Describing criminal justice legislation as a 'relentless' tidal wave, Sir Igor Judge noted that 'although it constantly comes in, unlike the tide it never seems to ebb'.[19] Even a cursory scan of the list of Home Office Acts introduced by the Blair and Brown governments (see Appendix IV) reveals the regularity with

---

[15] See Chris Huhne MP, *Hansard*, 4 December 2008, vol. 485 col. 171; A. Keogh, 'The Justice Merry-go-round', *New Law Journal*, 157 1037, July 2007; J.R. Spencer, 'The Drafting of Criminal Legislation: Need it be so Impenetrable?', *Cambridge Law Journal*, 67(3), November 2008, pp.585-605.

[16] This excludes Acts relating solely to Scotland or Northern Ireland, Acts that began life as private members' bills, and those related to criminal justice that were the primary responsibility of other departments, such as the Ministry of Justice.

[17] The Law Commission (2010), *Criminal Liability in Regulatory Contexts: An Overview, Consultation Paper No 195 (Overview)*, para.1.17, p.5.

[18] Rt. Hon The Lord Judge, Lord Mayor's Dinner for the Judiciary, Mansion House speech, 13 July 2010, p.4.

[19] I. Judge, 'Current Sentencing Issues', Lincoln's Inn, London, 29 October 2007, http://www.judiciary.gov.uk/docs/speeches/current_sentencing_issues_291007.pdf.

which certain policy areas have been legislated on over the period: for example, immigration in 1997, 1999, 2002, 2004, 2006, 2008 and 2009; and terrorism in 2000, 2001, 2005, 2006 and 2008. The Home Office has also introduced some particularly lengthy bills in recent years that have taxed the ability of Parliament to scrutinise them effectively. The Criminal Justice Act 2003, for example, contains 339 sections and 38 schedules, the Extradition Act 2003, 227 sections and four schedules, the Serious Organised Crime and Police Act 2005, 179 sections and 17 schedules, and the Nationality, Immigration and Asylum Act 2002, 164 sections and nine schedules. The demands on parliamentarians are thus perhaps greater than in the past if they are to have a clear understanding of what the bill actually entails and what its consequences might be given the size and complexity of the legislation before them. Some members in both Houses of Parliament readily admit that they frequently do not have a full grasp of the detail or the potential consequences of the technicalities of the legislation with which they are grappling.[20]

The Home Office record demonstrates, however, that the volume of legislation is not a new problem, and nor is it the product of the behaviour of any one particular party when in office. In 1996 the then lord chief justice, Lord Taylor, accused Conservative ministers of subjecting the law to 'arbitrary change and the vagaries of fashion', noting that there had been as many criminal justice acts in the previous six years as there had in the preceding 60.[21] Thirteen years later the outgoing lord chief justice, Lord Phillips, echoed this criticism, describing a 'ceaseless torrent of legislation, adding complexity to substantive law and to the sentencing exercise'.[22] Lord Phillips acknowledged that 'Some of this legislation is needed to deal with changing circumstances, and this includes some of the new terrorist offences... Other legislation is less easy to justify, including the subdivision of sexual offending into an astonishing number of different offences, some of which have yet to see the face of an indictment.'[23]

The consequence of these regular legal changes is increased complexity and difficulty for practitioners in the field. Marcel Berlins has argued that 'judges,

---

[20] See, for example, A. Brazier, S. Kalitowski & G. Rosenblatt with M. Korris (2008), *Law in the Making: Influence and Change in the Legislative Process* (London: Hansard Society), p.194.

[21] H. Mills, 'At war over the law', *The Independent*, 8 March 1996.

[22] The Court of Appeal Criminal Division (2009), *Review of the Legal Year 2007/2008*.

[23] *Ibid*.

lawyers, police and other experts in criminal justice [are] unable to keep up with the bewildering flow'. [24] And the House of Commons Justice Select Committee concluded in 2008 that: 'The sentencing regime has been complicated by both the pace and the volume of constantly changing legislation. In addition to dealing with new or short-lived criminal offences, sentencers are faced with Acts intended to simplify and clarify sentencing regimes that are themselves swiftly amended.' [25]

Attitude: political culture and disposition

The attitude of the executive to the legislative process contributes to and reinforces the problems in relation to the volume and quality of law being produced. Ministers increasingly assume that recourse to legislation, preferably a substantial flagship bill, is required for any policy. Any minister seeking to make his or her reputation and enhance their profile and influence aspires to a policy initiative, a white paper and a bill. Demand for slots in the government's legislative programme almost always exceeds supply and there is little evidence that the Cabinet's Parliamentary Business and Legislation Committee, which oversees the legislative programme, provides any rigorous internal controls to ensure that the government's proposed bills are properly prepared before introduction and that the policy proposals embodied in them have a clear legislative requirement. The media hardly helps this process by alleging that a minister has failed or lost out if he or she does not bring forward a large bill in each session.

The passage of a bill and the securing of Royal Assent is viewed as the primary test of a minister's political virility, regardless of whether the legislation ever actually achieves its stated aims or results in damaging unforeseen consequences. Such has been the regularity of ministerial reshuffles in recent years that ministers are rarely in position long enough to ever be preoccupied with the results of the legislation they have passed. Indeed, there is a strong link between the frequency of ministerial turnover and the likelihood of new policy and therefore legislative initiatives. A minister's average tenure in office prior to the Second World War was around four years; in the decades after the

---

[24] M. Berlins, 'Another fine mess we've got into, bad character and bad law, and legislation that spells chaos', *The Guardian*, 18 January 2005, G2 p.17.

[25] House of Commons Justice Select Committee (2007-08), *Towards Effective Sentencing*, HC 184, p.11.

war this reduced to about two years. More recently however, it has not been unusual for ministers to serve a year or less in post.

Change on such a regular scale inevitably impacts on the ability of ministers and civil servants to develop a coherent policy and legislative agenda and on the ability of external organisations to liaise with the relevant key personnel on that agenda and implement the departmental initiatives that arise.[26] This problem was powerfully illustrated by Sir Terence Etherton, Chair of the Law Commission, in a speech in 2007, when he set out some of the reasons why he believed the Law Commission had enjoyed less success than in previous decades in getting its recommendations considered by the government. In the 15 months since his appointment as Chair, there had, he said, 'been no fewer than four junior ministers in the Department of Constitutional Affairs/Ministry of Justice with responsibility for the Law Commission, that is to say averaging less than four months each. By contrast, experience has shown that it would be extremely difficult for the usual Law Commission project to be completed, with a draft bill, in under three years. This disparity between the life of a project and the movement of junior ministers within departments means that there can be no assumption that a project supported, and even promoted, by a department will be regarded with the same enthusiasm, or indeed any enthusiasm at its conclusion.'[27] Understandably then, when a new Home Secretary was announced in May 2007, a frustrated leader of the civil service union, the First Division Association, pleaded for stability and continuity: 'The next Home Secretary will be the fourth to hold that office in a three-year period. This leadership merry-go-round is destabilising, and the last thing the Home Office needs now is a new minister to walk in with a box of new priorities.'[28]

At its best, a reshuffle may ensure that the most able and trusted individuals are placed in the most important posts, thereby enhancing the quality of government as well as the authority of the Prime Minister. At their worst however, they can be highly expensive and cause serious disruption to the

---

[26] See House of Commons Public Administration Select Committee (2006-07), *Machinery of Government Changes*, HC 672; House of Commons Public Administration Select Committee (2008-09), *Good Government*, HC 97.

[27] Sir Terence Etherton, Chair, Law Commission, Bar Law Reform Committee Lecture, 'Law Reform in England and Wales: A Shattered Dream or Triumph of Political Vision?', 14 November 2007, pp.19-20.

[28] First Division Association Press Release, 'FDA concerned about Home Office leadership 'merry-go-round", 8 May 2007.

policy-making process. Political commentators have long argued that British political culture privileges change over expertise, that ministers are frequently inexperienced, lack the appropriate skills for the department to which they are allocated, and do not stay sufficiently long in post to build up the requisite technical policy knowledge and departmental memory required. The political process thus allows and encourages practices that would be seen as damaging and ineffective in virtually any other profession.

This is reinforced by similar weaknesses in civil service corporate memory. [29] Anecdotal evidence suggests that constant movement of personnel means that ministers and officials may simply forget or be unaware of legislation already in existence, and of policy initiatives and experiments that were considered, tried and discarded as unworkable or ineffective. The National Audit Office (NAO) found, for example, that in 1986 the then Department of Social Security passed an Act which restricted the access of state second pensioners' widows to benefits on the death of their spouse, the actual implementation of which was designed to come into force in 2002. However, in the intervening period the department simply 'forgot' about the change and pensioners and dependents were therefore misinformed about the benefits they would receive after 2002. The NAO estimated that the cost of this mistake was £5.5 billion. [30]

Once a bill passes into law the departmental or cross-departmental bill team that was formed to shepherd the policy proposal towards its legislative form is rapidly disbanded and dispersed. As one of our seminar participants put it, 'the civil service is like "Random Access Memory": it moves on after the job is done and forgets what it knew in the past'. There is clearly a need for mechanisms to ensure that the collective knowledge of the team is recorded and disseminated so that other bill teams in the future can learn the lessons of their experience. Without this commitment to evaluation and learning, poor ideas will keep being recycled into the legislative process. The development of a more robust system of post-legislative scrutiny may help in the process of evaluation. It was also suggested at one of our seminars that there needs to be much greater interaction between civil servants in departments and

---

[29] G. Lodge & S. Kalitowski (2007), *Innovations in Government: International perspectives on civil service reform* (London: IPPR), p.17.

[30] C. Gilson, P. Dunleavy & J. Tinkler (2008), *Organizational Learning in Government Sector Organisations: Literature Review* (London: LSE Public Policy Group), pp.21-22.

officials in Parliament. A number of participants indicated that knowledge about Parliament among civil servants today is generally poor; perhaps a result of the move from a culture of advice to a culture of operational service delivery in which, in the words of one participant, 'an educated understanding and respect for Parliament is not seen as a priority by those in the highest echelons of the civil service'. **Some form of short-term secondment or professional development training to raise levels of knowledge about Parliament and how it functions might therefore be useful for civil servants in the future.**

Ministers are also too often tempted to utilise their 'legislative opportunity' as a vehicle to take forward whatever policy ideas they may have at hand. As Lord Cope of Berkeley said of the Home Office, it 'seems to treat bills like buses: as soon as one has gone past they look to the next one…As soon as one arrives, the Home Office climbs on board with whatever luggage it happens to be carrying.'[31] What emerges from this process are 'Christmas Tree bills' on which hang a huge number of 'miscellaneous provisions' or omnibus bills which are, in effect, several bills in one, some of which are so large they have to be published in two parts. Ultimately, mammoth legislation such as the Criminal Justice Act 2003 is then 'bedevilled by contradictory goals and inconsistent principles'.[32] As Roberts noted, this particular Act exemplified the problem that 'modern English criminal legislation too often emerges from the parliamentary process looking like something the dog already ate for breakfast. Even setting aside the substance of the Act.....there are serious quality of law issues to be addressed.'[33] Another such Act was the Coroners and Justice Act 2009 where provisions related to topics ranging from assisted suicide and reform of the partial defences to murder, to measures to protect witness anonymity, bans on criminals profiting from publications about their crimes and extra powers for the information commissioner to penalise public and private sector bodies that lose personal data in addition to, as the short title reflects, reform of the death certification system. The bill's contents elicited much criticism in both Houses of Parliament with Lord Kingsland perhaps summing the concerns up best: '…the minister described this bill to your Lordships' House as 'wide-ranging'.

---

[31] Lord Cope of Berkley, *Hansard*, 8 July 2008, vol. 703 col. 704.

[32] 'Leader: Justice in Jeopardy', *The Guardian*, 22 November 2002.

[33] P. Roberts, 'Review: Blackstones' Guide to the Criminal Justice Act 2003', *International Journal of Evidence and Proof*, 9(2), 2005, pp.148-152.

We take the view that it could be broken up into several bills and that it would probably, as a consequence, get better scrutiny. I prefer to call this bill a miscellany or even a farrago, redolent of Mr Churchill's famous pudding.' [34] Robert Rogers, the Clerk Assistant of the House of Commons, confirmed at our seminar that omnibus bills such as this, which are 'in effect a convoy of disparate provisions', can pose real and practical problems in terms of scrutiny by members. This view is echoed by members themselves, such as Edward Garnier MP, who argue that such legislation is 'made for the convenience of the government and its civil servants' and 'is wholly impossible to scrutinise in the Commons'. [35]

If such bills also straddle departmental boundaries and are not cleared early enough with the other departments then this can compound the scrutiny problems. In 2008 for example, a Planning Bill was brought forward by the Department for Communities and Local Government but it did not consult with the other relevant departments – Business, Enterprise and Regulatory Reform and the Department of Environment, Food and Rural Affairs – until late in the day. As a result, just over 70 pages of late amendments of a largely technical nature had to be laid by the government at report stage to take account of these departmental concerns, in some instances amending amendments that had been agreed by members at the earlier committee stage. [36] This is clearly an unsatisfactory way to make law.

Legislation is perceived as a sign of action and therefore is a powerful public relations measure and communications tool; a heavy legislative programme suggests a breathless pace of reform, energy and endeavour. The generation of policy themes in the Queen's Speech has increasingly become an artificial communications exercise with legislative ideas brought forward to suggest a coherent overall package when in truth one does not exist. For example, it was reported at our seminar that there have been instances when the government's Legislative Programme Committee has proactively approached departments – for example, the Education Department – to demand that it bring forward a bill because educational themes were a key aspect of the government's strategic

---

[34] Lord Kingsland, *Hansard*, 18 May 2009, vol. 710 col. 1209.

[35] H. Porter, 'Labour's attack on Parliament invokes Henry VIII', *The Guardian*, 14 January 2009, http://www.guardian.co.uk/commentisfree/henryporter/2009/jan/14/statutory-instruments-parliament.

[36] House of Commons, *Hansard*, 25 June 2008, vol. 478 cols. 330-464.

focus and message. As a seminar participant noted, 'The Queen's Speech gives the government a day of news and then Parliament lives with the consequences for the rest of the year.'

Similarly MPs have described the government's use of the Home Office legislative programme as 'an extended press release' and commentators have argued that politicians believe 'that they can "fix" any problem – and placate any media outcry – by passing more laws'. [37] The Violent Crime Reduction Act was described as 'a needless bill... whose provisions are mainly duplicating legislation already in place but was cobbled together before the general election in May 2005 so that the government could show that it was dealing with the rise in violent crime, much of which appeared allied to the rise of binge drinking'. [38]

In an assessment of immigration policy during 10 years of the Labour government, Sarah Spencer asserts that Tony Blair and his successive home secretaries felt that the best way to reassure the public that they were addressing immigration and asylum concerns was to continually bring public attention to their tough policies, which came in a raft of bills. [39] Blair himself played a crucial role in pushing the government's agenda on asylum issues and 'consistently challenged the Home Office to do more'. [40] But a succession of Acts on the same subject can lead to provisions being superseded almost as soon as they are implemented and it is frequently impossible to distinguish the effects of one Act from another.

Ministers however, are not solely responsible for this state of affairs. They do not operate in a vacuum: they legislate to meet political and electoral imperatives, seeking to appeal to the fickle nature of public opinion and to sate the demands of a voracious round-the-clock media. When the government brought forward a modest legislative programme in the 2008 Queen's Speech (only 15 bills compared to 29 in 2007 and 25 in 2006) it was the subject of much media scorn, deemed 'thin' on legislation and, by extension, ideas. As the Hansard Society's Susanna Kalitowski noted at the

---

[37] G. Robson, 'Criminal Justice Legislation: An Ever Spreading Swamp', *Justice of the Peace*, 171 JPN 846, December 2007.

[38] G. Robson, 'The Madness of Governments', *Justice of the Peace*, 169 JPN 933, November 2005.

[39] S. Spencer (2007), 'Immigration', in A. Seldon (ed), *Blair's Britain, 1997-2007* (Cambridge: Cambridge University Press), p. 345.

[40] *Ibid.*, p.349.

time, it was a 'predictably cynical reaction' in a political culture where 'a large number of bills has become a sign of a government's strength, authority and capacity for innovation'. [41]

Preparation of legislation

Among the first questions that ought to be asked of any legislative proposal are is it necessary, and has it been technically well-prepared? Do the powers sought already exist in another Act on the statute book thus making new legislation superfluous? Can the issue be dealt with by administrative action alone? There is sometimes no justifiable rationale for recourse to making law in the first place but there are no clear restraints within government or Parliament to prevent it. There is no mechanism at present within the legislative process to simply evaluate and confirm the necessity of legislation or impose a quality standard on the production of a bill before it is sent to Parliament.

As Lord Norton notes, 'if deficient legislation is to be avoided, then there is a need to achieve greater constraint on the part of government, ensuring that legislation is necessary, well-prepared and subject to pre-legislative scrutiny. The ideal situation is compliance with all three criteria. Too often, the reality is compliance with one or none of them. To move towards the ideal requires a culture shift within departments and greater rigour on the part of Parliament to ensure that bills comply with these prerequisites.' [42]

Ideally, tackling unnecessary, duplicative or ill-prepared legislation would be dealt with up-stream in the legislative process at an early stage within departments. However, within government there is no one body or mechanism that has an explicit functional requirement to ensure that legislation is necessary and that it is well-prepared. The Cabinet Parliamentary Business and Legislation Committee, for example, does not adequately perform this checking and restraining function – its safeguards appear to be regularly bypassed for short-term political advantage – and whilst some departments have their own units that might provide it for their specific areas of legislative

---

[41] S. Kalitowski, 'More bills, please, we're British', *Our Kingdom*, 12 December 2008, http://www.opendemocracy.net/blog/ourkingdom-theme/susanna-kalitowski/2008/12/05/more-bills-please-we-re-british.

[42] Professor the Lord Norton of Louth, 'Bad Law: A Diagnosis', unpublished paper for the Hansard Society Making Better Law seminar, March 2009, pp.13-14.

interest, this offers only an *ad hoc* departmental approach when what is required is restraint embedded across government as a whole.

Parliament should therefore respond proactively to this problem for it is the one struggling with a near impossible workload. Barely able to keep its head above the legislative tidal wave, as a result, many parliamentarians are concerned about Parliament's capacity to effectively carry out its constitutional obligations in respect of legislative scrutiny. If there is no reason for the proposed legislation – or an aspect of the legislation – either because it duplicates legal provisions that already exist or because the problem or challenge can be resolved by non-legislative measures, might Parliament decline to consider it? The adoption of such a position would, of course, require a significant attitudinal shift among parliamentarians and there is little evidence that sufficient members of both Houses would be minded to move in this direction. Indeed, opponents of such an approach might justifiably argue that the elected government of the day has a right to implement its legislative programme.

However, the government surely does not possess an unfettered right to legislate. Parliament ought not actively to seek to prevent or unnecessarily defer the executive's legislative programme. But there is a strong case for establishing new ground rules to rebalance the legislative relationship between Parliament and government, establishing a consensual approach predicated on mutual acceptance of common standards of legislative consultation, preparation and scrutiny.

As a cross-party group of peers examining reform of the procedural practices of the Upper House recently stressed, Parliament has a right to expect that the government of the day will ensure that a bill is properly prepared, the policy objectives are clearly set out and the provisions are fit for purpose. [43] It noted damningly that at present, government 'does not always set out clearly enough the policy problem that is to be addressed through the provision of supportive evidence and analysis, the options that it has considered and the reasons for the choices it has made. The social and financial costs and benefits are not always set out, how a bill is to be implemented is often not defined, and the key challenges are sometimes not described.' [44]

---

[43] Report of the cross-party peers group on 'Improving scrutiny of primary legislation in the House of Lords', March 2010, p.1.

[44] *Ibid.*, p.2.

Parliament should at least be a partner in the process of setting the standards of what constitutes a validly prepared piece of legislation rather than permitting the executive to determine this from bill to bill. If parliamentarians are serious about checking the duplication of law and the growth of the statute book they must be both more imaginative and muscular in asserting their role and function *vis-à-vis* the executive.

The goal should be to build in some constraints – some checks and balances – to the legislative process at the parliamentary end such that they might restrain the executive from bringing forward hastily prepared, ill-thought-out legislation. A limited number of benchmarks – pre-introduction tests – that have to be met before legislation can proceed through Parliament might usefully help to offset the pressures caused by the impetus to legislate that bear down heavily at the Whitehall end of the process. In effect, Parliament needs a system to 'kitemark' bills, establishing standards of quality and best practice to demonstrate to MPs, peers and the public that the legislation being delivered is, at least in technical and procedural terms, fit for purpose, before it shifts to being considered in the political cauldron of both Commons and Lords where the policy issues can then be put to the test.

But how and on what basis would Parliament decide whether legislation was necessary and well-prepared? The Better Government Initiative has sought to outline some 'principles of good legislation' suggesting that once a policy has been decided and legislation is to be prepared then the following should be observed:

- 'Legislation should generally be avoided if the objective can be effectively and legitimately achieved by other means, or if the necessary powers exist already. The volume of new legislation should be kept to the necessary minimum.

- Legislation should be operationally necessary and should serve a substantive purpose. It should not normally be used for declaratory or symbolic purposes.

- It should be clearly expressed and unambiguous in its intention. It should avoid leaving areas of uncertainty which are likely to be contested and will have to be interpreted by the courts, possibly over a series of judgements and appeals.

- Any powers which it confers and any offences which it creates, together with the penalties for them, should be proportionate to the harm they are intended to prevent and restricted to the purpose for which they are intended.

- New criminal offences should be created sparingly and only when necessary for the rule of law. So far as possible, a bill should have a clear and coherent purpose or its purposes should be sufficiently connected to justify one bill.

- A bill should not duplicate existing legislation or particular powers which are already in force.

- Retrospective legislation should be avoided wherever possible.

- There should be clear criteria for the use of subordinate legislation, and a minister should not be able to amend primary legislation by Statutory Instrument ('Henry VIII clauses').

- Any exceptions should be fully justified and debated.

- Legislation on the same subject in several Acts should be consolidated.

- Bills should normally be published in draft to allow pre-legislative scrutiny.' [45]

This may not be a complete list, and some of the criteria will need more considered and detailed definition, but it certainly provides a useful starting point for discussions between government and Parliament if any agreement on common standards is to be reached.

A number of options present themselves if Parliament wishes to seriously tackle the problems of legislative volume and standards. Some of them it could pursue independently; others it would need to work in partnership with the government to achieve. It could agree to cap the number of bills it will consider from any single department over the course of a Parliament. An alternative approach would be to cap the number of bills it will consider from any single department before it requires that consolidating legislation be introduced. However, either approach might cause problems for some departments to a greater extent than others and might be deemed too arbitrary and blunt an instrument to deal with the problem. It could require that

---

[45] Better Government Initiative (2010), *Good Government: Reforming Parliament and the Executive, Recommendations from the Executive Committee of the Better Government Initiative* (London: Better Government Initiative), pp.20-21.

an individual or body within government must 'certify' to Parliament that the necessity of the bill and its technical quality has been evaluated and confirmed – this might be a minister or civil servant or both; or a relevant cabinet committee. It may provide for some restraint but there is a risk that a certification process quickly becomes nothing more than a 'tick box' exercise unless buttressed by other measures. This risk would be minimised if a parliamentary sifting committee, ideally established on a bi-cameral basis, then sat prior to second reading solely to evaluate the impact assessment and certification of each bill. Sifting committees – such as those that deal with delegated powers, human rights and constitutional issues – are well-established in Parliament and would therefore fit with the grain of current parliamentary processes.

But given the scale of the legislative tsunami that Parliament faces, a more radical departure is perhaps now justified. **A Legislative Standards Committee, ideally convened on a bi-cameral basis, could provide a gateway mechanism for assessing the necessity of legislation and whether the technical quality of a bill has met those standards Parliament has a right to expect and demand from government.** Empowered to call ministers to account before it and with the ultimate sanction to recommend to both Houses that they defer consideration of the bill because it does not meet mutually agreed qualifying standards of preparation, the existence of a Legislative Standards Committee would provide, over time, an important restraining influence on government and a further means to rebalance the relationship between Parliament and the executive. How such a committee might operate in practice is explored in greater detail in chapter 4. Suffice to say here that the risk to government of having a bill deferred by Parliament on the advice of the committee – in terms of reputational damage to ministers and officials and the general impact of delays to implementation of its legislative programme – would be a strong incentive for it rapidly to raise its game in this area. It would be for the government to demonstrate that it had met the agreed standards or, at the very least, made tangible attempts to do so.

Achieving high standards of legislative preparation cannot be divorced from the pressures that the volume of legislation and political disposition of ministers imposes on the drafting process. The size of the Parliamentary Counsel's office (those who are responsible for drafting primary legislation) remains relatively small despite increases in recent years. In 1997 there were

36 Parliamentary Counsel; today there are 60 with 22 support staff. [46] But, the size, scale and complexity of some bills mean that even these increased resources are stretched. Similarly, the tendency of government to re-write bills by tabling reams of amendments as they pass through Parliament, can rapidly absorb Counsel resources. As one participant in our seminar noted, it was not unusual for Parliamentary Counsel to finish drafting a bill one day only to begin working on a raft of amendments to it the next. The cumulative impact of this 'drafting on the hoof' is a negative one, for, as Rogers and Walters note, 'it occupies the time of parliamentary counsel, who could be working with a longer lead time on the next session's bills'. [47] As Robin Cook found, flagship bills that are the centre-piece of the government's programme may be being touted in public as imminent but work may not have begun in terms of drafting them. Recording his experience on becoming Leader of the House in 2001, he noted in his diary that the legislative programme appeared to have 'a bad case of broken jaw' as work had not even begun on 16 bills. 'I am taken aback on opening the cupboard door that I find the shelves so bare,' he wrote. [48] This is hardly an effective way to plan and manage the legislative process.

The legislative timetable

The cumulative impact of these difficulties in relation to volume, attitude and preparation are further compounded by the fact that legislation is dealt with through what Robin Cook described as a 'tidal wave' process rather than the 'pipeline' approach to which he aspired but was never able to achieve. [49] The legislative timetable is defined by annual sessions and although there is now provision for legislation to be carried over from one session to the next, this is rarely utilised, despite the fact that where it has been applied it has successfully facilitated improved scrutiny. Government much prefers the sessional cut-off because if a bill has not passed by the end of the session, it falls; it can thus use this justification to force through legislation towards the

---

[46] Office of the Parliamentary Counsel, 'Working with Parliamentary Counsel', 28 May 2010, pp.6-7, www.cabinetoffice.gov.uk/media/228366/wwpc%2028%20may%202010.pdf.

[47] R. Rogers & R. Walters (2006), *How Parliament Works*, 6th edition (London: Pearson/Longman), p.197.

[48] R. Cook (2003), *The Point of Departure* (London: Simon & Schuster), p.9.

[49] *Ibid.*, p.11.

end of the session. Conversely, the opposition likes the sessional cut-off because it can use the threat of a lost bill to push the government to make further concessions. The culture of party battle does not foster a spirit of dispassionate scrutiny.

The demand of ministers for legislative slots combines with an attachment to the sessional cut-off to create the tidal wave effect. Bills are introduced at the start of a session and go into committee at broadly the same time, thus creating 'peaks' and 'troughs' in scrutiny activity by parliamentarians. For MPs the workload is particularly heavy in February and March when a significant number of bills originating in the Commons go into committee, and again in June and July when bills arriving from the House of Lords have to be scrutinised. The impact of the tidal wave approach is particularly pronounced at the start of a Parliament, especially following a change in government at the general election, and then again at the end of the Parliament prior to dissolution for the next election.

The government's legislative programme is declared in the Queen's Speech within weeks of the convening of the parliamentary session after which there is then pressure to get a number of bills into the system, including the Finance Bill. For a new government that pressure is heightened by the sense that it must be seen to be actively delivering on its promises to the electorate and the timescales set out implicitly or explicitly in those promises. Thus, the current government quickly brought forward the Academies Bill following the May general election because it had pledged to allow schools to become academies by September 2010. In this instance the academy schools commitment transitioned from policy proposal, to drafting, to parliamentary scrutiny to the securing of Royal Assent in less than four months. Similarly the Parliamentary Voting System and Constituencies Bill 2010 was introduced in the summer on a timetable determined by the government's commitment to introduce a referendum on the voting system in May 2011 and to change the rules governing the determination of parliamentary constituency boundaries. As a consequence, the House of Commons Political and Constitutional Reform Select Committee did not have time to effectively scrutinise important constitutional proposals (as there were only two sitting days between presentation of the bill and second reading) prompting the committee to declare in its report on the legislation, 'We regret that it is being pushed through Parliament in a manner that limits both legislative and external scrutiny of its impact, and may consequently undermine the government's intention to restore the public's faith in Parliament.'[50]

These problems illustrate an essential difference between Parliament and government that impacts detrimentally on the law-making process but to which there is no obvious remedy. Simply put, Parliament and government operate to different timetables; the rhythm of their work is in conflict. Government requires relatively quick decisions and action to deliver demonstrable progress and change. On the other hand, in the words of Sir George Young MP, 'time is the oxygen of Parliament' but it is being 'suffocated' by the sheer volume of legislation arising from the scale and pace of government decision and action.[51] Parliament above all requires a reasonable amount of time at each stage of the scrutiny process for careful thought and detailed deliberation. But the process and procedures by which we currently make law do not always make sufficient provision for this.

The challenges in relation to time and deliberation are also acutely felt at the end of the Parliament during the 'wash-up' process when, in the few days between the calling of a general election and the dissolution of Parliament, outstanding legislation completes its passage through Parliament on an expedited timetable on the basis of deals made privately between the government and the main opposition party. The process restricts parliamentary scrutiny and marginalises backbenchers, minor parties and crossbench peers. A 'squalid stitch-up'[52], a 'rather sad and tawdry affair'[53], and a 'brazen disregard for Parliament'[54] were just some of the colourful descriptions of the 2010 wash-up.[55] It brings into sharp relief the concerns about legislative overreach by the executive coupled with manipulation of the parliamentary scrutiny process. To its defenders, the wash-up is a pragmatic if far from

---

[50] House of Commons Political and Constitutional Reform Select Committee (2010-11), *Parliamentary Voting System and Constituencies Bill*, HC 437, p.3.

[51] Sir George Young MP, 'Parliamentary Reform: The Conservative Perspective' lecture delivered on 18 March 2010, in Hansard Society (2010), *The Reform Challenge – Perspectives on Parliament: Past, Present and Future* (London: Hansard Society), p.52.

[52] Lord Tyler, *Hansard*, 7 April 2010, vol. 718 col. 1478.

[53] Evan Harris MP, *Hansard*, 8 April 2010, vol. 508 col. 1203.

[54] John Redwood MP, *Hansard*, 7 April 2010, vol. 508 cols. 1073-1074.

[55] See R. Fox & M. Korris, 'Reform of the Wash-up: Managing the Legislative Tidal Wave at the End of a Parliament', *Parliamentary Affairs*, 63(3), July 2010, pp.558-569.

perfect solution to the problem of how to bring parliamentary business to an orderly close in a way that enables the government not to lose valuable legislation upon which much time and resources have been spent. For its critics, however, the wash-up enables the government of the day to wait-out time in the final parliamentary session and then manipulate the process in order to evade scrutiny of the legislation before it reaches the statute book.

A more magnanimous reading of the process might conclude that each interpretation contains more than a grain of truth. If legislation were simply to hit the buffers on the announcement of a general election then valuable and useful bills or at least elements of them would be lost. As the acquiescence of the opposition party is required in order to get bills passed then it possesses not merely a restraint but a veto power over any controversial clause or bill. And though the process of negotiation in such a tight time frame is necessarily messy and imperfect as pragmatism clashes with principle, it does not automatically follow that it is detrimental to the public good and contrary to the interests of Parliament and the political process.

However, when a bill of major constitutional significance – such as the Constitutional Reform and Governance Bill – is included in the wash-up having been first introduced in the previous parliamentary session and then carried over, after earlier being subject to pre-legislative scrutiny, then the critics who condemn the government for abuse of the scrutiny process have considerable evidence to support their claims. Likewise, bringing forward the Digital Economy Bill late in the parliamentary session such that it received its second reading in the House of Commons only the day before the 2010 wash-up smacked at best of mismanagement of the legislative timetable, at worst of abusive disregard for democratic scrutiny and accountability. In similar vein, it is profoundly inadequate that an appropriations bill providing for a quarter of a trillion pounds of in-year public expenditure should be accepted with little or no consideration by the legislature in the dying hours of the Parliament.

If the current Fixed Term Parliaments Bill successfully completes its passage then this should change the nature of the parliamentary calendar and fix this 'wash-up' problem. But if the government is scrambling legislation through Parliament shortly before the next general election as it was during the 2010 pre-election wash-up then its reforms will have failed to bring any rationality to this aspect of the legislative system.

A growing culture of amendment

Throughout each parliamentary session the tidal wave impact interacts with the volume of legislation, the length and complexity of individual bills and the addition of late amendments in the legislative process to place significant demands on the capacity and resources of Parliament to scrutinise them effectively. In particular, the late addition of substantive government amendments to bills in progress and the increased use of delegated legislation are major obstacles to good scrutiny and significant contributory factors in the emergence of legislation that is constitutionally and procedurally deficient.

The number of amendments to bills made following introduction to Parliament has been on the increase for some years. Research by Blackburn and Kennon found that of bills introduced in the short 1996-97 session, their total size increased by about 10% as a result of the amendment process, and in the normal length 1999-2000 session, the size increased by 30% (from 2,700 to 3,600 pages). [56] In the 2007-08 session, there were 5,244 government amendments alone, evenly divided between both Houses (2,732 in the House of Commons and 2,512 in the House of Lords). At the time of our fourth and final seminar in October 2009, 2,274 amendments had already been laid during the session up to 17 July with a number of large bills still to proceed through their report and third reading stages in both Houses. One consequence of the scale of legislative amendments is that a significant on-going drafting commitment is required from Parliamentary Counsel.

The number of amendments should not automatically be seen as a guide to the intellectual or preparatory rigour of the legislative process. Some government amendments may be tabled in response to points made by MPs and peers on both government and opposition benches, or external comment from organisations or individuals during the passage of the bill. But the sheer scale of government amendments to its own legislation does suggest that something rather more serious is at work, particularly when amendments are tabled at report stage, often close to the tabling deadline, such that it is virtually impossible for members to scrutinise them effectively. When a bill such as the 2006-07 Planning Bill has 100 pages of government

---

[56] R. Blackburn & A. Kennon (eds) (2003), *Griffith & Ryle on Parliament: Functions, Practices and Procedures*, 2nd edition (London: Sweet & Maxwell), pp.6-150.

amendments tabled to it, then, in the absence of any other adequate explanation, one can reasonably conclude that something has gone awry in the preparation and drafting of the legislation. As Blackburn and Kennon noted, 'in many cases the legislative process is really a mechanism for the government of the day to tidy up under-prepared bills'. [57]

Not only do late amendments reduce the time available for scrutiny during the various stages of the legislative process, but they also constrain the ability of select committees and external groups to scrutinise the proposals. During the passage of the Home Office's Immigration, Asylum and Nationality Bill, for example, the government added 10 new clauses relating to counter-terrorism in the wake of the London bombings in July 2005. The amendments were announced on 15 September and published on 12 October, before receiving comparatively little time in the standing committee sessions from 18-27 October. [58] The Joint Committee on Human Rights (JCHR) published a report on 5 December 2005 condemning the counter-terrorism clauses as incompatible with international human rights law, but this was not until after the bill had completed its passage through the House of Commons. It was similarly criticised by the UN High Commissioner for Refugees. The clauses were on no occasion debated on the floor of the House of Commons, receiving scrutiny only in the un-elected House of Lords.

The impact of delegated legislation

An increasing reliance on delegated legislation, which is often tabled late or not at all during consideration of the parent bill, also results in deficient law. Delegated legislation provides many of the crucial powers and provisions not contained in primary legislation. Primary legislation often acts merely as a framework into which much of the real detail will subsequently be added through delegated legislation. This affects the quality of scrutiny that can be applied to the legislation for there are often significant disparities between the content of the discussion at the primary legislation stage and the final content of the delegated legislation. For example, during parliamentary

---

[57] *Ibid.*, pp.6-150.

[58] A. Brazier, S. Kalitowski & G. Rosenblatt with M. Korris (2008), *Law in the Making: Influence and Change in the Legislative Process* (London: Hansard Society), p.86.

debate on the Immigration, Asylum and Nationality Act 2006, ministers said that the fines for employers of illegal immigrants would be around £2,000; but in 2007, the government actually proposed that they could be up to £10,000.[59] The failure of government to provide parliamentarians with important SIs in draft for their consideration alongside the parent bill means that often there is a chasm between what MPs and peers are led to believe they are voting for and what is actually delivered. The problem is then compounded by the fact that SIs are subject to far less scrutiny than primary legislation. When they are laid before Parliament they are examined only once and are un-amendable, and it is therefore rare for either House to vote them down.

This situation is compounded by the increased use of Henry VIII clauses in legislation – provisions in a bill that enable primary legislation to be amended or repealed by SI, with or without further parliamentary scrutiny.[60] That these clauses are named after the 1539 Statute of Proclamations that gave Henry VIII the power to make law by proclamation should alert everyone to their dangers and the threat they pose to parliamentary sovereignty.

On the face of it, the inclusion of Henry VIII clauses do not make the law in which they are contained deficient – if the minister's intention is to secure broad-ranging powers to dis-apply statutory provisions at will then they perform their function. But they render the concept of parliamentary accountability and scrutiny in relation to a broad swathe of related legislation deficient and thereby undermine the constitutional foundations of the process by which law is made. For example, the 2008 Banking (Special Provisions) Act granted the Treasury the power to dis-apply any other statutes with a bearing on the provisions of the 2008 Act. It is estimated that 120 Henry VIII clauses were included in legislation in the 2009-10 parliamentary session alone.[61] Recent evidence suggests that this approach to the making of law is not the preserve of any one particular party but has become part of the natural culture of government. The new Conservative-Liberal Democrat coalition has introduced Henry VIII clauses to its Public

---

[59] *Ibid.*, p.196.

[60] House of Lords Select Committee on the Scrutiny of Delegated Powers (1992-93), *First report*, HL 57, para.10.

[61] Rt. Hon the Lord Judge, Lord Mayor's Dinner for the Judiciary, Mansion House speech, 13 July 2010, p.6.

Bodies Bill that, in the opinion of the Delegated Powers and Regulatory Reform Committee in the House of Lords, would 'grant to ministers unacceptable discretion to rewrite the statute book, with inadequate parliamentary scrutiny of, and control over, the process'.[62]

All the time in the world for scrutiny will not address these deficiencies in the legislative approach as long as the government can muster a parliamentary majority in favour of its bills. What is required is an attitudinal shift – a self-denying ordinance on the part of the government not to seek such powers so freely; and a greater willingness on the part of parliamentarians to resist the inclusion of such clauses in legislation in future, with mechanisms agreed and in place to restrain their use if government does not heed Parliament's concerns.

Streamlining the process

The problems at the start of a parliamentary session and then again at its close illustrate why a pipeline rather than tidal wave approach to legislation is so much more attractive. In reality however, the different work rhythms, demands and pressures facing Parliament and government mean that we are unlikely to see a shift to a pipeline approach anytime soon. But there is scope to streamline the law-making process through greater co-operation between government and Parliament to maximise their strengths, avoid duplicative work, and make best use of their resources in the interests of making better law.

That streamlining must begin at the start of the policy-making process within departments. Improved consultation processes in particular are crucial to this for they provide a means, through the deployment of expert evidence and advice, to root out problems with the legislation at an early stage and therefore give clearer guidance to legislative drafters about the aims and objectives of the policy. Theoretically at least, the more that problems are eradicated early on, the smoother the law's passage should be through the various government and parliamentary processes. Parliament's consultation processes could then better dovetail with those of government; if the consultation process at the departmental level is effective, then by the time the bill reaches Parliament the evidence base for it should be clear, allowing

---

[62] House of Lords Delegated Powers and Regulatory Reform Committee (2010-11), *5th Report – Public Bodies Bill*, HL 57.

Commons and Lords committees to focus on subjecting the policy case being made to detailed scrutiny. In practice, parliamentary committees often consult on the same issues dealt with earlier by government and as a result, the stakeholders with an interest in the matter – often the 'usual suspects' – are consequently subject to multiple consultation requests. There is a case for government making far more information, derived from its own consultation processes, available to parliamentary committees to aid their work. These issues are explored in greater detail in chapter 2. In practical terms, the more that the areas for potential conflict over policy can be narrowed down and clarified, the more that parliamentarians can then focus their resources and efforts on these most contentious areas of legislation, with scrutiny processes adapted accordingly to facilitate this shift in focus.

The ideal handling of legislation would see a three-stage scrutiny process undertaken for each and every bill: pre-legislative scrutiny; legislative scrutiny; and post-legislative scrutiny.

Pre-legislative scrutiny

Pre-legislative scrutiny of legislation in draft form by a select committee, or on occasion by a joint committee of both Houses, has been a useful innovative reform to the procedural process in the last decade. However, despite a commitment in 2003 that bills 'should be published in draft form unless there are good reasons for not doing so', over the years the number of bills subjected to pre-legislative scrutiny has declined. [63] Whilst there was early enthusiasm for pre-legislative scrutiny when Robin Cook MP was Leader of the House with 10 bills being considered in draft in both the 2002-03 and 2003-04 sessions, in the years since, the number of bills examined in draft has never numbered more than three with the single exception of the 2007-08 session (see Appendix V). Explaining the dearth of draft legislation, the then Leader of the House of Lords, Baroness Ashton, submitted to the Constitution Committee, that 'The main practical obstacle remains the need to have the freedom to bring forward much legislation on a timetable which does not allow for publication of the proposed legislation in draft form.' [64] Again, the issue of

---

[63] Phil Woolas MP, *Hansard*, 24 February 2004, vol. 418 col. 19 WH.

[64] House of Lords Constitution Committee (2007-08), *Pre-legislative Scrutiny in the 2006-07 Session: Follow Up*, HL 129, Appendix, p.4.

time, the volume of legislation, and the absence of a pipeline approach conspires against the interests of parliamentary scrutiny.

In practice, there are few reasons why government cannot bring forward legislation without first ensuring that it is subject to pre-legislative scrutiny. But to do so it must be prepared to initiate legislation at a slower pace and to plan more. Even where pre-legislative scrutiny has taken place government has often not allowed the recommended 12-week consultation period for it or responded in timely fashion to the findings of the committee. Given the increased scale and scope of legislation that now confronts parliamentarians, any curtailing of the pre-legislative scrutiny stage increases the risk that deficient legislation will not be properly addressed. On the face of it, the availability of time is the problem but in reality the problem is more of an attitudinal one. As Lord Carter commented to the Lords Constitution Committee, 'there are some departments, in fact all departments, that have people within them who do not like draft bills. They think the best thing to do is to produce the bill and then put it through the parliamentary process.'[65] And yet, where pre-legislative scrutiny has been utilised it has proven a useful tool for ministers and officials alike. Culturally, ministers have been more receptive to changing a bill at draft stage than they are once the bill has been tabled in Parliament. There is no obligation on the government to accept suggested changes but they do not tend to regard their acceptance as a political defeat. Less political capital is expended at the draft end of the law-making process. Indeed, it can often be politically advantageous to accept amendments at this stage as the bill may then secure a smoother and more expeditious passage later on. In contrast, once a bill enters the formal legislative process, ministers 'tend to adopt a proprietary attitude towards them'.[66]

Pre-legislative scrutiny is not without its challenges – not least the time constraints that impact on the legislative process and the additional burden of work it imposes on select committees. Nevertheless, the benefits of pre-legislative scrutiny outweigh the problems, many of which can be addressed by other procedural reforms adopted to streamline the process. Decisions

---

[65] House of Lords Constitution Committee (2003-04), *Parliament and the Legislative Process*, HL 173, para.26.

[66] *Ibid.*, para.10.

about which bills are subject to pre-legislative scrutiny currently lie entirely with the executive. **All bills ought to be examined in draft form; but in the absence of any commitment from government on this, an alternative approach would be for parliamentarians to determine criteria to assess which bills might be best suited for pre-legislative scrutiny and then agree, ideally on a bi-cameral basis, whether it should be dealt with by a committee in the Commons, the Lords, or by a Joint Committee of both Houses.** Again, the objective should be for Parliament to collectively assert more confidently and clearly what it deems to be minimally acceptable in relation to consideration of proposed laws in draft.

At the formal legislative stage, three key areas stand out where there is scope for reform and streamlining of the process to take account of the pressures that are inhibiting improved legislative scrutiny: programming, Public Bill Committees (PBCs), and a more bi-cameral approach in which the House of Commons and House of Lords work together more closely to avoid duplication of effort. Reform in each of these areas is tackled in greater detail in chapter 4 but it is important to appreciate the role that each can play in developing a more streamlined law-making process.

Programming

Programming motions are regarded as one of the most fundamental reforms undertaken in the House of Commons in the last decade. Programming motions outline the time that will be spent on each stage of the bill as it goes through the legislative process. When first implemented in 1998, the aim was to introduce more certainty into the legislative process and provide for greater scrutiny. In the early years of their operation there was political consensus between the parties but after 2001 this declined and programming motions have largely been carried by the government against the wishes of the opposition parties. As such, the process has become ever more controversial, with two particular criticisms levelled at it: that it strengthens the executive because it deprives the opposition of one of its rare parliamentary weapons, namely time, and therefore the ability to obstruct and delay legislation; and that the timetable is often so tight that a lot of legislation is passed entirely without scrutiny. For Labour's Tony Wright the process was 'guillotine by another name'; on the opposite side of the political divide, Conservative Sir Nicholas Winterton regarded it as a 'catastrophic disaster'.[67] As Sir Alan Haselhurst, a Deputy Speaker, noted in evidence to the Modernisation Committee, 'It was difficult to escape the conclusion that a reform which had originally been proposed as a way of securing a fair balance between the interests of the government, the opposition and other sections of the House, and ensuring adequate consideration of all parts of each bill had become just another weapon in the armoury for managing the business of the House.'[68]

An early Hansard Society assessment of programming in 2004 concluded: 'Programming was intended to eradicate or at least greatly reduce the gaps in scrutiny which occurred when time on a bill ran out, resulting in many important clauses being left un-debated. Programming is meant to be flexible but it is not always possible to predict in advance the time that will be needed to give full consideration to parts of the bill or predict which clauses will attract most attention or controversy.' And yet, 'despite the controversies and difficulties, programming has brought greater certainty, even rationality, to a legislative process that could previously appear bizarre and unpredictable.....Since in a programmed system, filibustering and delay simply reduce the time available for constructive debate, programming may discourage such practices.'[69]

The problems with programming or timetabling of parliamentary business are a good example of what can happen when a reform is introduced in isolation, decoupled from other reforms intended to accompany it as part of a broad package of change. When the Hansard Society's Commission on the Legislative Process (the Rippon Commission) recommended the introduction of timetabling, it saw this reform in the context of other proposed changes, namely greater use of pre-legislative scrutiny, the carry-over of legislation and the introduction of a Business Committee.[70] Modifications to the programming process could therefore now be made in the context of the introduction of a new Business Committee in three years' time, as promised by the coalition government, and a renewed commitment to pre-legislative scrutiny.

---

[67] A. Brazier, M. Flinders & D. McHugh (2005), *New Politics, New Parliament: A review of parliamentary modernisation since 1997* (London: Hansard Society), p.17.

[68] House of Commons Modernisation Committee (2001-02), *Modernisation of the House of Commons: A Reform Programme*, HC 1168, Appendix 42.

[69] A. Brazier (ed) (2004), *Parliament, Politics and Law Making. Issues and Developments in the Legislative Process*, (London: Hansard Society), p.25.

[70] Hansard Society (1993), *Making the Law: the Report of the Hansard Society Commission on the Legislative Process* (London: Hansard Society), chapter 7.

Public Bill Committees

Another recommendation of the Rippon Commission – the introduction of evidence taking Public Bill Committees to replace Standing Committees – was realised in the 2006-07 session. PBCs enable interested bodies and individuals to submit evidence to committees and so set their views on the public record, replacing their private communications with individual MPs which used to be the norm under the old committee system. In the words of Lord Norton, 'The convenience of interest groups is married with the public good of transparency.'[71] When working optimally the evidence sessions should allow MPs to engage with expert witnesses and through the course of detailed discussion to become better informed about the utility of the bill's provisions. However, again, the constraints of time imposed by the legislative timetable and the political and procedural constraints that currently govern the committee process conspire to undermine the potential of PBCs. The choice of witnesses called before the committee is in the control of the executive; the timing of committee sessions is often rushed with insufficient time for members to truly reflect on the import of the evidence they have heard; bills originating in the House of Lords are not eligible for consideration by a PBC; and the chairing of committee sessions is uneven at best. The advantages of PBCs are therefore not being fully realised at present. Chapter 4 sets out the reforms we believe are needed to rectify this, crucial to which would be the role of the proposed new Business Committee in providing for a more flexible approach to the timing of hearings. Again, streamlining could bring real benefits to the process.

But, given the problems facing Parliament with regard to the volume and standards of preparation of legislation, and the individual challenges parliamentarians face in properly understanding the legislation they are being asked to consider, there is a case for now taking a much more radical approach to committee work. Two possible approaches could be adopted. A new committee system could be established, at least on a trial basis, to combine the features of select committees and public bill committees as happens in the Scottish Parliament. Their use might improve both the quality of legislation and accountability through the development of the extra expertise that comes with the detailed knowledge of a subject area. Alternatively,

---

[71] Professor the Lord Norton of Louth, 'Bad Law: A Diagnosis', unpublished paper for the Hansard Society Making Better Law seminar, March 2009, p.9.

specialist committees could be created to look at all legislation – in draft or full form – within a certain legislative area. These would have the advantage of injecting the select committees' more collegiate and consensual mode of working into PBCs which remain a more adversarial form of committee work.

There is also much scope for an array of reforms to procedures in the House of Lords to 'more effectively harness and deploy the expertise in the Upper House for the purposes of legislative scrutiny whilst wherever possible avoiding duplications of work already undertaken by the House of Commons'.[72] Viewing the scrutiny process on a bi-cameral, parliamentary basis in which the work undertaken by peers supplements but does not duplicate that undertaken by MPs (and vice-versa) would help to rationalise and prioritise consideration of legislative proposals and offset some of the pressures caused by their volume, size and scale. Peers should have a role in the gateway Legislative Standards Committee, in establishing criteria for pre-legislative scrutiny of bills, in communicating more clearly their concerns about key clauses and amendments to MPs once the bill transitions from one House to the other, in holding their own public evidence hearings at committee stage, and in post-legislative scrutiny.

If we are to make better law in the future it is essential that the laws we do make are also reviewed following implementation so that they can be revised if necessary in order to meet their objectives, but also to learn the lessons from the process by which they were created. The securing of Royal Assent should not mark the end of the legislative process.

Post-legislative scrutiny

Following a recommendation from the House of Lords Constitution Committee that most Acts, other than Finance Acts, should be reviewed within three years of commencement or six years following enactment, whichever was sooner, the government referred the matter to the Law Commission for consideration.[73] Its 2006 report endorsed the recommendation and suggested a Joint Committee on Post-Legislative Scrutiny be established for the purpose.[74] The government

---

[72] Report of the cross-party peers group on 'Improving scrutiny of primary legislation in the House of Lords', March 2010, p.1.

[73] House of Lords Constitution Committee (2003-04), *Parliament and the Legislative Process*, HL 173, p.44.

[74] The Law Commission (2006), *Post-Legislative Scrutiny*, LC No. 302, Cm 6945, paras 6.6-6.11.

has since accepted that Acts should be reviewed between three and five years after enactment but that the burden of work should lie with departmental select committees who will be tasked with considering their relevant department's reviews.[75] However, the initiation of that review process remains with the executive. As Toulson noted, it will 'require an attitudinal shift to make the best use of this development. Successive governments have subscribed to the idea in theory... But in practice, governments have always had other priorities. The problem is not so much one of lack of parliamentary time as lack of departmental time and commitment.' [76]

Post-legislative review may over time become for government the norm rather than the exception but for Parliament there are two fundamental challenges that must be addressed. Firstly, whether and how it can wrest initiation of the process from government by establishing a more consensual approach to this aspect of the scrutiny process; and secondly, how it can then ensure adequate scrutiny of the reviews. Select committees already face a heavy workload and therefore finding time for post-legislative scrutiny may not be a priority. **A dedicated Post-Legislative Scrutiny Committee, ideally constituted on a bi-cameral basis, might be a more effective approach and would facilitate the development of expertise in this complex area of the study of law and its consequences. Alternatively, some form of joint sifting committee could be established to prioritise which aspects of an Act will be reviewed in order to rationalise the post-legislative scrutiny process.**

---

[75] Office of the Leader of the House of Commons (2008), *Post-Legislative Scrutiny: The Government's Approach*, Cm 7320.

[76] R. Toulson, 'Forty Years On: What Progress in Delivering Accessible and Principled Criminal Law?', *Statute Law Review*, 27(61), June 2006.

Chapter 2: Moving from policy to law: the role of external expertise

The volume and increasingly complex technical nature of legislation heightens the need for effective and early engagement and consultation with external policy experts who can contribute to the development of a strong evidence base for policy development purposes. The explosive proliferation of knowledge and information, and the myriad ways in which it is now produced and disseminated, means it is increasingly difficult for both government and Parliament to collate, manage and interpret the information they need to inform the policy-making and legislative process. Effective use of external expertise can play a role in helping to address this challenge.

Consultation at a formative stage also needs to take place with those who will be directly affected by the proposed policy and resulting statute and SIs. As Needham concluded, 'Governments need to involve those groups whose compliance is required for policy enforcement – a concern which was as relevant for a monarch consulting with feudal lords to secure the collection of taxes as it is for [the current] government in relation to pressure groups over policy reform.' [77]

The Rippon Commission identified three key areas of departmental decision-making during the course of preparation of a bill:

- Identification of a problem that may require a legislative solution and determination of the relevant facts;

- Clarification of the policy options and choice of policy to be followed;

- Determination of the methods by which the policy should be applied and the consequential practical questions that result. [78]

At each stage there is scope for engagement with external experts and advisers, and at a minimum, in the event that ministers are reluctant to consult

---

[77] C. Needham, 'Consultation and Local Government', *Parliamentary Affairs*, 55(4), October 2002, pp.699-714.

[78] Hansard Society (1993), *Making the Law: the Report of the Hansard Society Commission on the Legislative Process* (London: Hansard Society), pp.33-34.

on those aspects they regard as the political objectives of the legislation, there is room for consultation on how those objectives can best be achieved.

Optimal consultation – early and thorough in scope – should help inform policy development in such a way that it improves the efficacy of the legislation that emerges by 'providing a check on whether the proposed measure is technically adequate for its purposes, and whether it might have unforeseen and unacceptable side effects'. [79] It should thus help provide better direction to Parliamentary Counsel by ministers and officials and should ultimately lighten the load on Parliament in the later legislative stages by minimising the need for on-going amendment and re-drafting due to original imperfections that could and should have been avoided. The passage of legislation through both Houses of Parliament might thus be less adversarial and more constructive.

At present, however, views about the efficacy and value of the consultation processes are decidedly mixed, both within government and externally among stakeholders. While they can exert a noticeable influence on legislation, there is evidence of increased cynicism among consultees; an impression exists in some quarters that the process does not always 'seem genuine'. [80] There are concerns about how experts who trade in evidence, particularly in academia, are engaged in the policy development process and the pressures that emerge as a result of the differing approaches to professional method and practice between these experts and those who occupy the political sphere. The degree to which 'evidence' and 'opinion' may be too readily conflated and evidence ignored for political reasons is a source of real tension.

This chapter explores these issues in more detail, looking at how specialist and expert input might improve legislation, particularly through the injection of empirical research into the system. It analyses how the consultation and subsequent policy and legislative development process might better encourage and utilise expert advice, and identifies a number of innovative mechanisms that might facilitate that input in the future.

---

[79] *Ibid.*, p.17.

[80] A. Brazier, S. Kalitowski & G. Rosenblatt with M. Korris (2008), *Law in the Making: Influence and Change in the Legislative Process* (London: Hansard Society), pp.177-178.

The roots of consultation

Until the mid-1960s, government consultation with outside bodies was largely carried out on an informal basis or through meetings of small groups or advisory bodies. Consultation documents, when they were used, were 'normally limited to individuals and organisations most immediately concerned'. [81] This changed in 1967 with the publication of the first green paper that invited public discussion on regional economic policy. [82] Explanations for the change vary: ministers argued that the new approach was in the interests of greater openness and would facilitate public participation; others argue that there is little evidence that ministers were seized by these arguments, being motivated primarily by pragmatism following recent criticism of the hurried and secretive manner in which they had been developing policy and legislation. [83] An alternative analysis is that the move towards greater participation in policy-making arose in the context of growing criticism of professional experts during the socially turbulent periods of the 1960s and 1970s. 'Critics frequently used phrases like the "tyranny of expertise" and "conspiracy against society"', argues Fischer. 'Not only were experts accused of failing to generate solutions relevant to the diverse range of interests in society as a whole, they were charged with using their professional authority and technocratic methods to buffer power elites against political challenges from below.' [84]

Whatever the reason, since 1967 there has been an explosion in formal consultation undertaken by government. At the time of our seminar on the role of external expertise in 2009 it was estimated that 173 departmental consultations were underway. In recent years the number of consultations has been known to reach 500 or more, with some departments, particularly those with a strong regulatory role, for example the Department for

---

[81] A. Silkin, 'Green Papers and Changing Methods of Consultation in British Government', *Public Administration*, 51(4), Winter 1973, pp.427-48.

[82] HM Treasury (1967), *The Development Areas: A Proposal for a Regional Employment Premium* (London: HMSO).

[83] See C. Needham, 'Consultation and Local Government', *Parliamentary Affairs*, 55(4), October 2002, pp.699-714 and A. Silkin, 'Green Papers and Changing Methods of Consultation in British Government', *Public Administration*, 51(4), Winter 1973, pp.427-48.

[84] F. Fischer, 'Citizen participation and the democratization of policy expertise', *Policy Sciences*, 26(3), 1993, pp.165-187.

Environment, Food and Rural Affairs, being responsible for over 100 in any given year. [85]

But what we are seeing is perhaps an increasing reliance on general stakeholder responses, prioritising opinion over evidence from those with a wide variety of skills and knowledge, often from interested parties such as campaign and pressure groups. Their engagement in the process addresses in many instances the need to consult about the impact and implementation of policy and legislative proposals. But what we are not seeing to the same degree is an increase in the involvement of technical experts from further afield, particularly from academia, who may be more disinterested and less aligned with sectoral interests of a political or policy kind and better placed to provide advice and support in respect of the evidence base for policy development. What is needed is a more judicious balance that secures more effective engagement of a broader, more diverse range of experts.

The purpose and conduct of consultation

In examining government consultations as part of the policy-making process that leads to law it is useful to consider the various purposes for which consultation is employed. A useful analysis of this issue is provided by Walters, Aydelotte and Miller who suggest five broad governmental objectives when consultation is embarked upon, namely:

i.   *Discovery* — a search for definitions, alternatives, or criteria.

ii. *Education* — to inform and educate the public about an issue and proposed alternatives.

iii. *Measurement* — to assess public opinion on a set of options.

iv. *Persuasion* — to persuade the public toward a preferred option.

v.   *Legitimisation* — to comply with public norms or legal requirements. [86]

---

[85] See for example the analysis of public consultation by government departments in 2006 in W. Grant & M. Rush, 'Demands and Responses: Pressure Politics in 2007-08', in M. Rush & P. Giddings (2008), *When Gordon Took the Helm* (Basingstoke: Palgrave Macmillan), p.73.

[86] L.C. Walters, J. Aydelotte & J. Miller, 'Putting More Public in Policy Analysis', *Public Administration Review*, 60(4), July/August 2000, pp.349-59.

These definitions can also be placed alongside the timescale of policy development, for good consultation requires asking the right people the right questions at the right time. *Discovery* takes place at the earliest stage, where policy is undeveloped and intentions may still be vague; *education*, where the intended will may be clear, but policies to implement it are unformed; *measurement*, where policy ideas have been fleshed out but no final decision on a course of action has yet been taken; *persuasion*, where a policy has been decided upon and is unlikely to change, and *legitimisation*, where the decisions have been taken and the consultation is simply a matter of going through the motions. The purpose of a government consultation and the point in the policy-making process that it occurs will therefore naturally go hand-in-hand.

Unsurprisingly external stakeholders strongly prefer consultation to take place as early in the policy-making process as possible. [87] With policy still in flux it gives outsiders a greater chance of making their voice heard and influencing the final decision. Once a proposal is on the table the politics and the dynamics of the consultation process inevitably change; ministers and civil servants become more proprietorial towards it.

There is evidence to suggest that early consultation can reap valuable rewards for government. The case studies examined by the Hansard Society for its study of *Law in the Making* highlighted the fact that extensive consultation over a number of years had taken place prior to the introduction of the 2001 Export Control Bill, the 2005 Equality Bill and the 2006 Welfare Reform Bill, and that these had influenced policy and contributed to smoother and more consensual passages of all three bills through Parliament. [88]

The green paper on strategic export controls broadly corresponded to the *discovery* definition, as it invited comments 'on all aspects of strategic export controls procedures and policy, and on the statutory basis of export control', posed a number of open-ended questions, and marked the start of a process that would lead to further consultation on a white paper. [89] The green paper

---

[87] Hansard Society (1993), *Making the Law: the Report of the Hansard Society Commission on the Legislative Process* (London: Hansard Society), p.21; A. Brazier, S. Kalitowski & G. Rosenblatt with M. Korris (2008), *Law in the Making: Influence and Change in the Legislative Process* (London: Hansard Society), p.135.

[88] A. Brazier, S. Kalitowski & G. Rosenblatt with M. Korris (2008), *Law in the Making: Influence and Change in the Legislative Process* (London: Hansard Society), pp.177-178.

[89] Department for Trade and Industry (1996), *Strategic Export Controls – A Consultation Document*, Cm 3349, para.1.2.

preceding the Equality Bill fits the *measurement* definition, in that it provided three options for reform of Britain's equality institutions, although there was an element of *persuasion* in that the government had expressed a preference for one of them (the Single Equality Body model). [90] The welfare reform green paper combined elements of *discovery*, *education* and *measurement*. It set out the challenges in the welfare system as it currently saw them, sought opinions on its suggested solutions, and asked for other ideas to help address the challenges. [91]

The greatest problems and criticisms appear to arise in relation to consultations that fall into the *persuasion* and *legitimisation* categories. The Cabinet Office consultation that prepared the way for the Legislative and Regulatory Reform Bill, for example, was subsequently condemned by the House of Commons Regulatory Reform Committee for including leading questions and being short on detail. [92] This is far from a new critique: in evidence to the Hansard Society Commission in 1993 the Consumers' Association noted that consultation 'can be a genuine request for help, or merely an attempt to legitimise proposals that the government has already made up its mind to pass into law'. [93]

There is an extent to which such criticisms may stem from false expectations of the consultation process. As Kane and Bishop note, 'consultation is sometimes popularly interpreted as a peculiar form of direct democracy involving contingent segments of the public. Rather than being seen as a means through which policy may (hopefully) be influenced, it is seen as a means by which policy may be mutually determined.' [94] False expectations or leading consultations are far from ideal for both government and consultees. Not only do they reduce the value of the responses received, but they

---

[90] Department for Trade and Industry (2002), *Equality and Diversity: Making it Happen*; Department for Trade and Industry (2002), *Equality and Diversity: The Way Ahead*.

[91] Department for Work and Pensions (2006), *A new deal for welfare: Empowering people to work*, Cm 6730.

[92] House of Commons Regulatory Reform Committee (2005-06), *Legislative and Regulatory Reform Bill*, HC 878.

[93] Hansard Society (1993), *Making the Law: the Report of the Hansard Society Commission on the Legislative Process*, (London: Hansard Society), p.18.

[94] J. Kane & P. Bishop, 'Consultation and Contest: The Danger of Mixing Modes', *Australian Journal of Public Administration*, 61(1), March 2002, pp.87-94.

undermine the faith of those being consulted, who can become jaundiced and dispirited by a process which they feel, rightly or wrongly, is not working transparently and fairly.

An example of this dilemma can be seen in the 2007 consultation on a third runway for Heathrow Airport, which was described as 'heavily biased'[95] and 'a complete sham'[96] by opposition parties and campaigners, who subsequently launched a legal challenge to the consultation arguing that it was unlawful. The judge ruled that the consultation 'did not seek responses relating to the principle of development' as the government's support had been long-established in the 2003 *The Future of Air Transport* white paper. However, an evolving legal argument by the opposed groups eventually succeeded in contesting the government's decision not to re-examine the policy commitment, given the intervening time and the significance of the policy and implications of the Climate Change Act 2008 and Planning Act 2008.[97]

While earlier consultation is clearly preferable, consultations at the *persuasion/legitimisation* end of the scale are not inherently without value or purpose. There will naturally be occasions when government has decided on a policy and needs either to persuade the public that its chosen course of action is correct, or consult on the fine detail around it. However, it is in the presentation of the government's position that improvements need to be made. Wherever possible, consultation documents should clearly set out which elements of a proposal can be changed and which are fixed.[98] While this will not eradicate complaints, a more open and honest approach may help generate a more productive atmosphere and better results.

To this end, there needs to be greater adherence to the government's own *Code of practice on written consultation*. The development of such a code was suggested by the Hansard Society in 1993 following detailed consideration of government consultation processes by the Commission on the Legislative

[95] Greenpeace, *Airfixed! Why the government's consultation on Heathrow is a sham*, 25 January 2008, http://www.greenpeace.org.uk/blog/climate/airfixed-the-governments-sham-consultation-on-heathrow-20080125.

[96] Theresa Villiers MP, *Hansard*, 2 April 2008, vol. 474 col. 850.

[97] R (on the application of London Borough of Hillingdon and others) v Secretary of State for Transport, [2010] EWHC 626 (Admin).

[98] Hansard Society (1993), *Making the Law: the Report of the Hansard Society Commission on the Legislative Process* (London: Hansard Society), p.35.

Process. The Commission concluded that 'the government should, drawing on best practice, prepare consultation guidelines which would be applicable to all government departments when preparing legislation'. [99] Seven years later, in 2000, the Prime Minister launched the *Code of practice on written consultation*, setting out seven criteria for all government consultations. [100] These were updated in January 2004 [101] and again in November 2008 [102] and currently read as follows:

i. *When to consult*

Formal consultation should take place at a stage when there is scope to influence the policy outcome.

ii. *Duration of consultation exercises*

Consultations should normally last for at least 12 weeks with consideration given to longer timescales where feasible and sensible.

iii. *Clarity of scope and impact*

Consultation documents should be clear about the consultation process, what is being proposed, the scope to influence and the expected costs and benefits of the proposals.

iv. *Accessibility of consultation exercises*

Consultation exercises should be designed to be accessible to, and clearly targeted at, those people the exercise is intended to reach.

v. *The burden of consultation*

Keeping the burden of consultation to a minimum is essential if consultations are to be effective and if consultees' buy-in to the process is to be obtained.

---

[99] *Ibid.*, p.39.

[100] Cabinet Office (2000), *Code of practice on written consultation*, http://archive.cabinetoffice.gov.uk/servicefirst/2000/consult/code/_consultation.pdf.

[101] Better Regulation Executive (2004), *Code of Practice on Consultation*, http://webarchive.nationalarchives.gov.uk/20060213220102/http://www.cabinetoffice.gov.uk/regulatio n/consultation/documents/pdf/code.pdf.

[102] HM Government (2008), *Code of Practice on Consultation*, www.berr.gov.uk/files/file47158.pdf.

vi. *Responsiveness of consultation exercises*

Consultation responses should be analysed carefully and clear feedback should be provided to participants following the consultation.

vii. *Capacity to consult*

Officials running consultations should seek guidance in how to run an effective consultation exercise and share what they have learned from the experience.

In its 2008 annual review, the Better Regulation Executive (BRE) declared that the revised Code 'should lead to noticeable improvements in how government consults'.[103] However, previous research by the Hansard Society has found that departmental observance of the Code has been inconsistent and opaque [104] and, as Professor the Lord Norton of Louth has highlighted, the government does not have an overarching system for monitoring and enforcing it. [105]

The one element of the Code that does receive some scrutiny is adherence to the recommended 12-week duration of consultations, the results of which are often published in departmental annual reports. Compliance in this regard appears to be patchy. While 80% of consultations on statutory instruments lasted 12 weeks in 2005, this fell to 75% in 2006. [106] For all consultations by 11 government departments in 2009, only 71% lasted at least 12 weeks (though for five other departments reporting in 2008-09 the figure was 79%). The Code requires that any consultation that falls short must receive ministerial approval, and while some departments publish the reasons for failing to meet the requirements, others do not. There will inevitably be cases when external factors necessitate a short timescale, or where the issue being consulted on is sufficiently specific and well-defined as to easily facilitate consultation with all relevant parties. That around one quarter of all consultations do not, however, adhere to the guidance suggests that the good practice of the Code is not

---

[103] Better Regulation Executive (2008), *Making it Simple: Annual Review 2008*, www.berr.gov.uk/files/file49780.pdf.

[104] R. Ferguson (2006; 2007), *Digital Dialogues, Interim and Second Phase Reports* (London: Hansard Society/Ministry of Justice).

[105] Lord Norton of Louth, *Hansard*, 14 May 2009, vol. 710 col. GC496.

[106] House of Lords Merits of Statutory Instruments Committee (2007-08), *The Management of Secondary Legislation: follow-up*, HL 70, p.5.

sufficiently embedded across government and that more work is required to ensure that it is taken more seriously.

Audience and impact

The audience for government consultations varies widely. While the consultation on strategic export controls received just 38 responses [107] and one on veterinary medicines 57 responses, [108] a consultation on genetically-modified crops generated 11,000 responses, [109] and the consultation on a third runway for Heathrow attracted almost 70,000 responses. [110]

Numbers of course do not tell the whole story. A large response is certainly no guarantee of good quality feedback, and a small one may be the result of narrowly-drawn, highly technical or specialised subject matter, about which few people are willing or able to respond. [111] Alternatively, it may be that a consultation has been designed too much with particular stakeholder groups in mind, or with the aim of producing a particular set of responses. [112]

What follows a consultation in terms of analysis of results and feedback is equally as important as the consultation process itself. As the Merits of Statutory Instruments Committee in the House of Lords has made clear, analysis of the results of consultation is vital for good policy-making and proper scrutiny: 'The analysis of a consultation exercise is not an afterthought but should drive policy.' [113]

---

[107] A. Brazier, S. Kalitowski & G. Rosenblatt with M. Korris (2008), *Law in the Making: Influence and Change in the Legislative Process* (London: Hansard Society), p.21.

[108] Department for the Environment, Food and Rural Affairs (2008), *Summary of responses to the consultation on the future of the Veterinary Medicines Directorate (VMD)*, http://www.defra.gov.uk/corporate/consult/vmd-future/summary-responses.pdf.

[109] Department for the Environment, Food and Rural Affairs (2007), *Summary of responses to Defra consultation paper on proposals for managing the coexistence of GM, conventional and organic crops* (London: Department for the Environment, Food and Rural Affairs), p.1.

[110] Ipsos MORI & Detica (2008), *Adding Capacity at Heathrow Airport: Report on consultation responses* (London: Department for Transport), p.24.

[111] A. Brazier, S. Kalitowski & G. Rosenblatt with M. Korris (2008), *Law in the Making: Influence and Change in the Legislative Process* (London: Hansard Society), p.39.

[112] *Ibid.*, pp.177-178.

[113] House of Lords Merits of Statutory Instruments Committee (2007-08), *The Management of Secondary Legislation: follow-up*, HL 70, p.7

There are longstanding complaints from consultees that the feedback from consultations is insufficient. The 1993 Rippon Commission concluded that feedback should be 'maximised' and that, 'Analyses showing the degrees of support for the various proposals put out by departments are desirable. The government's own reactions to the response they had received, including explanations why rejected ideas could not be accepted, should usually be published.'[114]

While other recommendations, such as publishing the submissions received for a consultation, have been taken forward, poor feedback continues to be a problem, dispiriting consultees and undermining trust in the process. The Cabinet Office/Better Regulation Executive consultation on *Effective Consultation* reported that 'feedback, in several people's eyes, is key to trust in the process and key to future engagement', and concluded that future consultations 'should place greater emphasis on the feedback government provides following consultation exercises, and that wherever possible it should go beyond summarising the views heard during the consultation exercise by stating how the responses to the consultation will affect policy development.'[115]

However, the government still has some way to go to address this challenge. The Better Government Initiative has recently re-emphasised this point, arguing that government should provide a detailed account of the 'final conclusions on the policy to be adopted and how it is to be implemented, and preferably explain why the government has not accepted any widely supported arguments put to it during the consultation process. It should enable parliamentarians and other interested parties and groups to have sufficient understanding of any proposed legislation or policy and why it was chosen in preference to other means, with specific information about its social, local or economic effect on different groups.'[116]

Identifying the impact of consultations can be challenging, in part as a result of the different purposes for which they are used, but also because the views of participants, even on an individual consultation, can vary markedly. Appraising

---

[114] Hansard Society (1993), *Making the Law: the Report of the Hansard Society Commission on the Legislative Process*, (London: Hansard Society), p.35.

[115] Better Regulation Executive (2007), *Effective Consultation: Government response* (London: Department for Business, Enterprise & Regulatory Reform), p.17.

[116] Better Government Initiative (2010), *Good Government: Reforming Parliament and the Executive* (London: Better Government Initiative), pp.12-13.

the consultation on strategic export controls, one NGO representative argued that 'the consultation gave the "impression of change", but for the most part the "substance changed very little" and in some cases "deteriorated."' [117] However a respondent from another NGO asserted that a number of welcome changes had been made during the consultation process. [118] *Law in the Making* concluded, having looked in detail at five very different legislative case studies, that whilst consultation can make a difference to individual elements of a policy, it is unlikely to change the general direction of that policy even if the views expressed in consultation are overwhelmingly opposed. [119]

Greater openness and transparency in the policy development process, with more opportunities to see how it is developing and what are the factors changing it, may go some way to ameliorate this negative perception. The Hansard Society has found in the past that feedback compliance and quality varies greatly across departments, [120] and is often only a broad-brush summary of responses. This could be markedly improved by departments releasing full copies and transcripts of consultation responses and the data sheets compiled to influence decision-making, and by making greater efforts to respond specifically to the evidence received and to acknowledge where suggestions had been incorporated into policy. Making the full range of consultation material available – including all submissions – if requested to do so by a parliamentary committee might also be useful in supporting scrutiny of policy by the Commons and Lords at a later stage of the law-making process.

It should be of real concern within government that there is now a growing level of cynicism about the consultation process, and the extent to which it is seen by stakeholders to be 'genuine'. While some departments have built up a reputation for regular and robust consultation, others are considered less effective or well disposed toward gathering stakeholder input beyond 'trusted circles'; some make use of all the resources available, while others are perceived merely to be going through the motions. [121]

---

[117] A. Brazier, S. Kalitowski & G. Rosenblatt with M. Korris (2008), *Law in the Making: Influence and Change in the Legislative Process* (London: Hansard Society), p.39.

[118] *Ibid.*

[119] *Ibid.*, pp.177-178.

[120] Hansard Society (2007), *Evidence to the Cabinet Office consultation on Effective Consultation*, http://www.hansardsociety.org.uk/files/folders/2007/download.aspx

[121] *Ibid.*

There is a tendency for those undertaking consultation to reach out repeatedly to the same set of stakeholders; the well-known practitioners, commentators or researchers in the field. There is obviously validity in seeking the views of these individuals and groups, and it can be integral to the success of legislation to have the support of the well-known names.[122] However an over-reliance on the 'usual suspects' risks limiting the breadth of views and evidence contributed, and adds little to the debate.

There is also an underlying battle for control of stakeholder opinion, which risks politicising and/or alienating experts. Once individuals or groups become identified through regular media appearances as key spokespeople on a particular area of policy, government and others (including third sector organisations) will seek to bring them 'on side' in preparation for future policy announcements or campaigns. There is a fear of being sucked into the policy process that may undermine their independence; some researchers find their contributions have been seen to be politicised and therefore they are considered to be less able to provide an objective approach.

Improving consultation

To improve the consultation process fundamentally, a number of reforms are now needed.

Consultations on legislation should be more structured, and should be focused much more clearly on choices and priorities, taking respondents through competing arguments and the consequences of each choice.

The often unrealistic approach of suggesting that all options are open – even when it is obvious that the government has a clear direction in mind – should be avoided. Being straightforward about what can or cannot change as result of consultation would bring greater confidence to the system.

There is scope for greater use of consultation evidence to strengthen parliamentary scrutiny. There should be more detailed feedback presented to Parliament and the public, in the form of reports on

---

[122] See discussion of the Welfare Reform Act 2007 in A. Brazier, S. Kalitowski & G. Rosenblatt with M. Korris (2008), *Law in the Making: Influence and Change in the Legislative Process* (London: Hansard Society), p.135.

consultation undertaken for every bill (draft or full). Such reports, in addition to summarising the consultation evidence, should address specific points and evidence rather than just present a broad-brush response, and give the reasons why certain proposals were chosen and others rejected. Although it may not be practicable in those rare instances when consultations receive tens of thousands of submissions, wherever possible in all other circumstances the government should aim to publish all the responses received to consultations. **And if Parliament requests it, specific submissions or indeed the complete set of evidence should be provided to facilitate their own committee consultation processes.** [123]

Underpinning these reforms the government should also take steps to ensure greater monitoring and enforcement of the use of the *Code of practice on consultation* by individual departments with a view to embedding it in the culture of departmental work.

Finally, the Merits of Statutory Instruments Committee recommendation that **greater efforts should be made to consult thoroughly on secondary legislation** should be heeded. As the Committee points out, statutory instruments are often not subject to debate and cannot be amended, and 'it is thus vital that Parliament can assure itself that the initiating department has made every effort to ensure that the instrument laid before the House is fully fit for its stated purpose'. [124] Given the limitations in scrutiny of delegated legislation, there is as great a need for advance consultation and expert input into the formation of secondary legislation as for its primary counterpart. Possible models for facilitating improved consultation on secondary legislation are set out towards the end of this chapter.

Academic and technical expertise: integrating research evidence and policy development

There is an important distinction to be made between consultation on a policy proposal and research regarding that policy proposal. Consultation is the collection and aggregation usually of opinion as much as evidence, often on a

---

[123] *Ibid.*, p.203.

[124] House of Lords Merits of Statutory Instruments Committee (2007-08), *The Management of Secondary Legislation: follow-up*, HL 70, p.4

relatively short timescale. It is comparatively cheap and short-term. Research on the other hand is slower and more expensive, but can provide a better evidence base for decisions about policy development, objectives, implementation and outcomes than a public consultation is able to provide.

However, research experts across a range of disciplines simply do not have the engagement with and impact upon the policy process that some of their international counterparts take for granted. British researchers are perceived largely to be removed from the political sphere, resulting, as Dejevsky argues, 'in a class of academics that is not as good as it should be at communicating outside its own discipline – and politicians and government departments that keep to themselves'. [125]

The Council for Science and Technology acknowledges that for the scientific community 'engagement between academics and policy-makers in the UK is not as strong as it might be', [126] while the British Academy have 'serious concerns that policy-makers are not realising the full potential of the contributions that humanities and social science research can make to public policy-making'. [127] Both bodies have highlighted how research evidence could and should have a more integral role in policy development. [128]

Over the past 10 years, successive governments have recognised the need for better engagement with researchers. Indeed, the phrase 'evidence-based policy making' became a mantra for ministerial speeches and government documents. The 1999 white paper, *Modernising Government*, for example, stated: 'This government expects more of policy-makers. More new ideas, more willingness to question inherited ways of doing things, better use of evidence and research in policy-making and better focus on policies that will deliver long-term goals.'[129]

---

[125] M. Dejevsky, 'The US relies on experts – the British just ignore them', *The Independent*, 28 April 2009.

[126] Council for Science and Technology (2008), *How academia and government can work together* (London: Council for Science and Technology), p.3.

[127] British Academy (2008), *Punching our weight: the humanities and social sciences in public policy making* (London: British Academy), p.iii.

[128] See Council for Science and Technology (2008), *How academia and government can work together* (London: Council for Science and Technology), p.3; S. Nutley, J. Percy-Smith & W. Solesbury (2003), *Models of research impact: a cross sector review of literature and practice* (London: Learning and Skills Research Centre), p.40; British Academy (2008), *Punching our weight: the humanities and social sciences in public policy making* (London: British Academy), p.27.

[129] Cabinet Office (1999), *Modernising Government*, Cm 4310.

The Cabinet Office's 2001 report, *Better Policy-Making,* sets out an evidence-based approach to public policy development predicated on reviewing existing research; commissioning new research; consulting experts and/or using internal and external consultants; and considering a wide range of properly costed and appraised options. [130]

The use of scientific evidence by government departments has, however, proven a particular minefield and the guidelines on its use have consequently been updated several times – in 1997, 2005 and again in June 2010. They now suggest that departments and policy-makers should:

- 'identify early the issues which need scientific and engineering advice and where public engagement is appropriate;

- draw on a wide range of expert advice sources, particularly when there is uncertainty;

- adopt an open and transparent approach to the scientific advisory process and publish the evidence and analysis as soon as possible;

- explain publicly the reasons for policy decisions, particularly when the decision appears to be inconsistent with scientific advice; and

- work collectively to ensure a joined-up approach throughout government to integrating scientific and engineering evidence and advice into policy-making.' [131]

So, given this focus within government on the importance of evidence-based policy, what accounts for the serious disconnect between academic expertise and policy-makers?

The first problem lies with the way in which politicians and policy-makers evaluate, weigh and differentiate between opinion and evidence. The weighing up of opinion is a task that politicians must naturally undertake before taking their decisions, but ensuring that the evidence is clearly separated and evaluated beforehand is crucial. While opinion is comparatively easy to assess, scrutinising evidence – particularly evidence that challenges a proposed policy direction – is a more time and resource intensive process and a greater

---

[130] Centre for Management and Policy Studies, Cabinet Office (2001), *Better Policy-Making.*

[131] Government Office for Science (June 2010), *The Government Chief Scientific Adviser's Guidelines on the Use of Scientific and Engineering Advice in Policy Making,* pp.3-4.

challenge. There is a belief among policy experts, articulated clearly at our seminars, that civil servants find it hard to evaluate the credibility of evidence, and that evidence-based objections to a policy are consequently often lumped together with opposed opinion submissions and rejected without explanation or engagement with the arguments made.

There is also a problem in relation to the 'terms of engagement' between policy-makers and expert advisers. This is a particular challenge in relation to scientific evidence and advice as was demonstrated by the reaction to comments by Professor David Nutt, chairman of the government's Advisory Council on the Misuse of Drugs (ACMD). Professor Nutt was sacked in October 2009 by then Home Secretary, Alan Johnson MP, for arguing in a lecture that alcohol was more harmful than illegal drugs such as ecstasy and cannabis. [132] Johnson accused Nutt of 'campaigning against government policy', [133] despite the fact that Nutt's lecture had been given in his professional capacity as Professor of Neuropsychopharmacology at Imperial College, London and appeared to conform to the government's code of practice for scientific advisers. [134] Nutt's sacking prompted five other members of the ACMD to resign within a fortnight. [135] When the government then announced amendments to its guidelines setting out the terms of engagement between ministers and their expert advisers, another member left arguing that they would compromise scientific independence. [136]

Another controversial case of science clashing with government is the subject of homeopathy. The House of Commons Science and Technology Select Committee published a report in February 2010 which concluded that the NHS should cease funding homeopathy treatment and that the Medicines and Healthcare Products Regulatory Agency (MHRA) should not license homeopathic products, on the basis that 'the systematic reviews and meta-

---

[132] M. Tran, 'Government drug adviser David Nutt sacked', *The Guardian*, 30 October 2009.

[133] S. Jones & R. Booth, 'David Nutt's sacking provokes mass revolt against Alan Johnson', *The Guardian*, 1 November 2009.

[134] M. Henderson, 'David Nutt's controversial lecture conformed to government guidelines', *The Times*, 2 November 2009.

[135] T. Whitehead, 'Three more drug advisers quit over sacking of Professor David Nutt', *The Daily Telegraph*, 10 November 2009.

[136] I. Sample, 'Meow meow' review may be hampered after drug adviser quits in scientific objectivity row', *The Guardian*, 29 March 2010.

analyses conclusively demonstrate that homeopathic products perform no better than placebos'. [137] However, the government's reply in July 2010, while acknowledging the weakness of evidence for homeopathy, concluded that it would not withdraw it from the NHS on the basis that to do so would limit patient choice and undermine its attempts to devolve power to a lower level. [138] This was despite the 'grave concerns' of the government's Chief Scientific Adviser, [139] and previous statements by both the governing coalition parties in support of strong evidence-based science policy. [140]

The challenge is, of course, that government may solicit advice and evidence but it is not compelled to heed it. Other factors in policy development and decision-making also have to be factored into their thinking, not least long-held values, political convictions and electoral imperatives, which do not necessarily bear down on the research community. But the goodwill and respect of researchers is squandered when politicians who make decisions contrary to clear evidence do not then explain clearly and openly why they have chosen to disregard that evidence. As the House of Commons Science and Technology Committee concluded, 'There will be many situations in which policy is primarily driven by factors other than evidence, be they political commitments or judgments (e.g. the minimum wage), moral standpoints (e.g. stem cell research), or urgent responses to circumstances or policies on which there is little empirical evidence to go on...Where there is an absence of evidence, or even when the government is knowingly contradicting the evidence - maybe for very good reason – this should be openly acknowledged.' [141]

There are also concerns among research experts that policy-makers seek evidence to fit with a pre-determined policy direction. The Council for Science and Technology identifies that the 'prime cause of mistrust or hostility amongst academics is a sense that in some cases they are being brought in on tight

---

[137] House of Commons Science and Technology Committee (2009-10), *Evidence Check 2: Homeopathy*, HC 45, p.19.

[138] Department of Health (July 2010), *Government Response to the Science and Technology Committee report 'Evidence Check 2: Homeopathy'*, Cm 7914.

[139] S. Connor, 'Government ignored our advice on homeopathic remedies, say experts', *The Independent*, 3 August 2010.

[140] M. Robbins, 'Conservative science policy ticks (nearly) all the right boxes', *The Guardian*, 28 April 2010; M. Robbins, 'Liberal Democrats: Science test results', *The Guardian*, 26 April 2010.

[141] House of Commons Science & Technology Committee (2005-06), *Scientific advice, risk and evidence based policy making*, HC 900, p.47.

timescales to support the answer that government wants to hear – characterised as "policy-based evidence"'. [142] The House of Commons Science and Technology committee argues that 'If evidence-based policy-making is to retain credibility, it is essential that it is not abused: ministers should only use the phrase when appropriate and need not be too chary about acknowledging that certain policies are not based on evidence. They should certainly not seek selectively to pick pieces of evidence which support an already agreed policy, or even commission research in order to produce a justification for policy: so-called "policy-based evidence making".' [143]

However, there are serious concerns, especially when government is directly managing and funding research, that unhelpful findings are suppressed. Boden and Epstein go as far as to argue that the routines of 'evidence-based policy' are 'fundamentally flawed by virtue of the fact that government, in its broadest sense, seeks to capture and control the knowledge-producing processes to the point where this type of "research" might best be described as "policy-based evidence"'. [144] This critique has been particularly levelled at the Home Office under successive Conservative and Labour governments, with accusations that research that was not 100% supportive of government policy would not be published and that papers were shelved or withdrawn from conferences on the insistence of ministers. [145]

The guidelines issued by the Government Office for Science are clear on the importance of scientific freedom: 'In public presentations, departments should wherever possible consider giving experts (internal or external) a leading role in explaining their advice on a particular issue. Independent scientific advisory bodies should have the ability to communicate relevant advice freely, subject to normal confidentiality restrictions, including when it has not been accepted.' [146]

---

[142] Council for Science and Technology (2008), *How academia and government can work together* (London: Council for Science and Technology), p.10.

[143] House of Commons Science & Technology Committee (2005-06), *Scientific advice, risk and evidence based policy making*, HC 900, p.47.

[144] R. Boden & D. Epstein, 'Managing the research imagination? Globalisation and research in higher education', *Globalisation, Societies and Education*, 4(2), July 2006, pp.223-236.

[145] S. Tombs & D. Whyte, 'Why bad news is no news and crime is big business', *Times Higher Education Supplement*, 21 November 2003.

[146] Government Office for Science (June 2010), *The Government Chief Scientific Adviser's Guidelines on the Use of Scientific and Engineering Advice in Policy Making*, p.11.

It is essential that these guidelines are respected by both sides in order to ensure the effective engagement of researchers and utilisation of evidence.

Policy-makers of course have their own reasons for finding engagement with the research community difficult. As former Permanent Secretary Lord Bichard said at our seminar, excessive dependence on expertise risks a narrowing of thought, incrementalism, and timidity in the face of major policy challenges or social or economic crises. Sometimes politicians and policy-makers simply have to make judgements based on incomplete evidence, particularly when doing nothing is not an option.

When they do access it, policy-makers often find academic research, 'frustratingly hedged around with caveats so that it does not offer a clear message'.[147] The rapid production of information is also changing perceptions among policy-makers about what constitutes evidence and expertise with less reliance being placed on the traditional professional communities who have hitherto been seen 'as the proper agents' for supporting and sometimes 'policing' policy-makers – as well as being occasional sources of innovation.[148] Too much research, particularly in the social sciences, is perceived to be obscurely focused and irrelevant to many of the challenges with which government is grappling.

There is between the two groups a significant communication chasm: policy-makers struggle to articulate what they want from researchers in policy and evidence terms; whilst researchers are often unable or unwilling to tailor their explanations to the policy context.

Models for engagement between researchers and policy-makers

How then can the vital exchange of research and evidence between research experts and policy-makers be facilitated in the interests of making better law?

Civil servants should take a more pro-active approach to the commissioning of research based on long-term policy direction,

---

[147] Lord Bichard, 'Moving from policy to law: the role of external expertise', unpublished paper for the Hansard Society Making Better Law seminar, June 2009, p.2.

[148] *Ibid.*, p.1.

identifying and promoting to academics those priority areas where research would most aid their strategic policy development work.[149] It is suggested, however, that the commissioning process should be different from the contractual process by which studies are purchased from professional consultants. As the British Academy emphasises, 'a good commissioning process should involve an element of peer review' and not just competitive tendering.[150]

Another option would be for all government departments to establish 'Analytical Research Contact Units' with a dedicated remit to find, engage and commission research from academics to inform the work of departmental civil servants and help with long-term policy development. As the Better Government Initiative stresses, 'The capacity of departments to construct and review their policies through the use of structured consultation and expert research and analysis needs to be safeguarded and strengthened. Those with a policy development function should have a strong technical capacity of their own and effective links to academics and practitioners outside government and to overseas experts.'[151]

In the scientific field some government departments already have dedicated independent Scientific Advisory Councils (SACs) to help manage their relationship with the science community[152] and more than 70 Scientific Advisory Committees exist to provide advice on particular scientific issues. While these are primarily aimed at the hard sciences, the Scientific Advisory Council at DEFRA has a social science sub-committee to engage with a broader range of research and this model could be replicated more widely.

An alternative approach would be to encourage greater support for the development of 'co-production' models for research, where researchers and policy-makers engage throughout the research process so that both sides have a better understanding of the needs

---

[149] British Academy (2008), *Punching our weight: the humanities and social sciences in public policy making* (London: British Academy), p.xi.

[150] *Ibid.*, p.x.

[151] Better Government Initiative (2010), *Good Government: Reforming Parliament and the Executive* (London: Better Government Initiative), p.13.

[152] The Departments with SACs are Department for Culture, Media and Sport, Department for the Environment, Food and Rural Affairs, Food Standards Agency, Home Office and Ministry of Defence.

and workings of the other, and thereby produce more valuable outcomes. [153] During our seminar, the National Institute for Health Research Service Delivery and Organisation Programme was held up as an exemplar of good practice in this field. It was established in 1999 to consolidate and develop the evidence base on the organisation, management and delivery of health services, and to promote the uptake and application of that evidence in policy and practice. [154] Today it focuses on 'commissioning research evidence that improves practice in relation to the organisation and delivery of healthcare'; on 'building research capability and capacity amongst those who manage, organise and deliver services – improving their understanding of the research literature and how to use research evidence', and consults widely to identify the most important research questions to which the NHS needs answers. [155]

Secondments, sabbaticals and professional exchange programmes offer alternative short-term opportunities for researchers and policy-makers to enter each other's professional territory and immerse themselves in their differing work environments and culture. Senior civil servants are, for example, now being offered six-week sabbaticals at the London School of Economics to reflect on their work in partnership with leading academics in the social sciences. In the other direction, the Economic and Social Research Council has funded an academic placement in the Government's Social Research Unit, based in the Treasury. The post was first filled in 2009 by Professor Philip Cowley, Professor of Parliamentary Government at the University of Nottingham, who spent nine months working in the Treasury, in a role he has described as 'pimping for academics', as he worked to develop routes to encourage better engagement between social scientists and government. That these initiatives are relatively novel and quite limited in scale suggests that there remains much scope for building more diverse partnerships of this kind in the future. Similar solutions involving better communication and learning processes are also needed between policy-

---

[153] British Academy (2008), *Punching our weight: the humanities and social sciences in public policy making* (London: British Academy), p.43.

[154] National Institute for Health Research, 'History of the SDO Programme', http://www.sdo.nihr.ac.uk/historyofthesdoprogramme.html.

[155] National Institute for Health Research, 'Welcome to the SDO Programme', http://www.sdo.nihr.ac.uk/index.html.

makers and front-line staff and practitioners to feed better ideas and experiences into the policy-making process. The National School of Government has expressed concern that there are only 'isolated examples' of good front-line policy engagement when what is needed is an 'integrated joined-up strategy'. [156]

Given the explosion in the availability of information and the ways in which it can be disseminated, coupled with concerns about the communication chasm between researchers and policy-makers, the opportunities around the concept of knowledge brokers and policy entrepreneurs should be explored. Officials could actively establish closer links with organisations such as research bodies or independent think-tanks, who can act as knowledge brokers (effectively middle-men) with the wider research community, or act as policy entrepreneurs in instances where they have the flexibility to experiment, test and develop new policy ideas. The skill set and experience of the brokers/entrepreneurs would be such that they could effectively be able to straddle the different worlds of policy and academia. Capable of understanding both the culture and methods of the research community as well as the procedural and political demands of government, they would be positioned to synthesise information and communicate it accurately to both sides. As Lord Bichard suggested, 'This work falls somewhere between the worlds of research, special advisers and other civil servants – a space where those involved in government can access the latest thinking tailored to their needs.' [157]

Further thought also needs to be given to how best to engage with experts who might provide helpful research evidence through traditional professional bodies. These bodies themselves claim that they are 'often overlooked when it comes to making complex, technical policy decisions relevant to their fields of expertise'. [158] Comparing their profile in the policy and parliamentary spheres, they find they fare less well than the top professional services firms and institutional bodies such as the Trades Union

---

[156] Sunningdale Institute (2009), *Engagement and Aspiration: Reconnecting Policy Making with Front Line Professionals* (London: Cabinet Office), p.6.

[157] Lord Bichard, 'Moving from policy to law: the role of external expertise', unpublished paper for the Hansard Society Making Better Law seminar, June 2009, p.2.

[158] Spada (2009), *British Professions Today – The State of the Sector* (London: Spada Ltd), p.28.

Congress (TUC) and Confederation of British Industry (CBI). Attitudes to professional bodies and associations may have changed among officials within government departments as a result of changing attitudes to evidence and expertise and the proliferation of sources and access to knowledge and information. However, professional bodies can provide technical expertise for the purposes of policy development and often front-line experience of policy implementation. Government's approach to the stakeholder status of professional bodies would benefit from further review.

Working with experts on the front line of service delivery, policy-makers should also consider greater piloting of proposals wherever possible in order to provide insight and a clear evidence base for legislative changes. The Pathways to Work and local housing allowance pathfinder pilot projects that preceded the Welfare Reform Act 2007 provided a substantial evidence base that facilitated a comparatively smooth passage for the legislation through Parliament. [159] Providing that clear ethical guidelines and standards of practice are put in place there is considerable scope to expand the use of such pilots and involve researchers and professional bodies in their development and evaluation. [160]

Finally, an example of good practice for improving evidence-based analysis of legislative proposals – the Social Security Advisory Committee (SSAC) – should be replicated in other technically complex areas of policy. Established in 1980 as a statutory body, it provides expert, independent advice to the Secretary of State for Work and Pensions on the often complex and technical issues of social security. Its primary function is the scrutiny of social security regulations proposed by the Department for Work and Pensions (DWP) and the social security-related benefits – such as Tax Credits and Child Benefit – administered by Her Majesty's Revenue and Customs (HMRC). The legislation covering the SSAC places a duty on the Secretary of State for Work and Pensions to refer all relevant proposals to the SSAC for consideration ahead of implementation, thereby guaranteeing the

---

[159] A. Brazier, S. Kalitowski & G. Rosenblatt with M. Korris (2008), *Law in the Making: Influence and Change in the Legislative Process* (London: Hansard Society), pp.131-133.

[160] Social Security Advisory Committee (2007), Occasional Paper No.2, *An examination of the ethical and legal issues of 'piloting' in its widest sense in the Department for Work and Pensions*, http://www.ssac.org.uk/pdf/occasional/piloting_paper.pdf.

SSAC's involvement in the scrutiny process. The committee also has a role in considering equality and diversity issues in proposed regulations, scrutinising the information products produced by the DWP, and generally giving advice on social security issues as it sees fit. [161] It is rare among advisory Non-Departmental Public Bodies (NDPBs) in having legislative scrutiny as a core part of its function. While a small number of other advisory NDPBs are also statutorily required to advise on legislation, such as the Industrial Injuries Advisory Council, their remit tends to be much more specific or in areas subject to less legislation, and therefore the legislative scrutiny element of their work is a small fraction of that involving the SSAC.

Led by a Chair appointed by the Secretary of State, a further 10 to 13 experts are appointed to the SSAC from a variety of specified backgrounds. One member is appointed after consultation with the TUC, another with the CBI, and one after advice from Northern Ireland. One member must be either disabled and/or in a position to represent the interests of disabled people and, by custom, one member is resident in Wales, one in Scotland and at least one member is from an ethnic minority.

In scrutinising regulations the committee may issue consultation documents, hold stakeholder meetings and go on visits to assist their deliberations. The SSAC submits a report to the Secretary of State, who will usually publish it along with the government's response as a Command Paper at the time of laying the regulations. While the government is required to consult the SSAC, it is not compelled to accept their recommendations, but in cases where the committee's advice is not followed it often leads to their concerns being aired in Parliament, particularly by the House of Lords Committee on the Merits of Statutory Instruments (the Merits Committee). [162] The SSAC itself estimates that historically around 60% of their recommendations have been accepted, [163]

---

[161] Social Security Advisory Committee (2008), *Twenty First Report – August 2007-July 2008*, http://www.ssac.org.uk/pdf/reports/21streport.pdf.

[162] See for example, House of Lords Merits of Statutory Instruments Committee (2007-08), *Drawing special attention to: Energy Performance of Buildings (Certificates and Inspections) (England and Wales) (Amendment No. 2) Regulations 2008, Social Security (Miscellaneous Amendments) (No. 4) Regulations 2008, Bradford & Bingley plc Transfer of Securities and Property etc. Order 2008*, HL 171, pp.3-6; Lord Kirkwood of Kirkhope, *Hansard*, 18 June 2007, vol. 693 col. 76; House of Lords, *Hansard*, 10 November 2008, vol. 705, cols. 504-523.

[163] Paper by SSAC Secretariat, cited in H. Genn (May 2004), *Report of the Quinquennial Review of The Social Security Advisory Committee (SSAC)* (Department for Work and Pensions), Cm 6189, p.20.

although analysis of the response to recent advice from the SSAC suggests that the government was not as accommodating in the last five years as it had been previously. [164]

The independent Quinquennial Review of the SSAC carried out by Professor Hazel Genn in 2004 also noted the importance of the SSAC's informal, behind-the-scenes influence. It was deemed to play a 'very important role through informal discussions prior to the laying of regulations in influencing the Department' and although this influence might not be visible and transparent its 'existence and continuing dialogue' with the Department was recognised by those working in the field. [165] The House of Commons Work and Pensions Select Committee has been particularly positive about the quality of the SSAC's work, praising it for providing 'expert, impartial advice in an area of legislation which might become a rather dark corner if it were not for the occasional floodlight emanating from SSAC'. [166]

Delegated legislation is a particularly complex, little understood, and rarely scrutinised area of law-making but given the growth in the volume of SIs now emanating from government there is a need to provide parliamentarians with greater support and expertise to scrutinise it. A significant flaw in the SSAC model is that its remit does not extend to delegated legislation passed within six months of relevant primary legislation. However, if this flaw were addressed, the SSAC model could be utilised in other policy-making areas where there is a similar reliance on complex secondary legislation. [167]

A recent initiative which is not dissimilar to the SSAC model is the emergence of the new Banking Liaison Panel to advise the Treasury on statutory

---

[164] SI 2009/604: The Social Security (Claims and Payments) Amendment Regulations 2009; SI 2009/609: The Social Security (Transitional Payments) Regulations 2009; SI 2009/614: The Housing Benefit Amendment Regulations 2009; SI 2009/480: The Social Security (Flexible New Deal) Regulations 2009; Draft Social Security (Lone Parents and Miscellaneous Amendments) Regulations 2008; SI 2008/2424: The Social Security (Miscellaneous Amendments) (no.4) Regulations 2008; SI 2007/1331: The Social Security, Housing Benefit and Council Tax Benefit (Miscellaneous Amendments); SI 2006/3188: The Social Security (Claims and Payments) Amendment (No.2) Regulations 2006; SI 2005/3: The Social Security (Incapacity Benefit Work-focused Interviews) Amendment Regulations 2005; The Draft Social Security (Incapacity for Work) (General) Amendment Regulations 2003.

[165] H. Genn (May 2004), *Report of the Quinquennial Review of The Social Security Advisory Committee (SSAC)* (Department for Work and Pensions), Cm 6189, p.20.

[166] House of Commons Work and Pensions Committee (2002-03), *Social Security Advisory Committee*, HC 296.

[167] A. Brazier, S. Kalitowski & G. Rosenblatt with M. Korris (2008), *Law in the Making: Influence and Change in the Legislative Process* (London: Hansard Society), p.149.

instruments made under the Banking Act 2009, as well as the special resolution regime, the banking code of practice and any other matters referred to it by the Treasury. One member of the panel is appointed by each of the Treasury, the Bank of England, the Financial Services Authority, and the scheme manager of the Financial Services Compensations Scheme. One or more members must also be appointed who, in the Treasury's opinion, represent the interests of the banks, are experts in law regarding UK financial systems and are experts in insolvency law and practice. [168] It is too early to assess and evaluate the efficacy of the Panel but, like the SSAC, it provides a model that might be rolled out to embrace other policy areas where the scale of law-making through delegated powers is particularly high.

The development of new procedural models like the SSAC or the Banking Liaison Panel offer the prospect that valuable technical expertise and insight might be applied to the making of laws across a much larger swathe of government than is presently the case. But will government be willing to establish new NDPBs at a time when it is trying to reduce the number of quangos? If the procedural problems associated with the proliferation, drafting and scrutiny of delegated legislation persist then the need for such bodies will grow and even if Parliament were to change the way it scrutinises SIs, it would still need informed advice to maximise the effectiveness of that scrutiny process.

Ultimately, however, procedural and structural changes alone will not be enough. If the integration of external and expert advice into the policy development process is to improve then cultural and attitudinal changes are also required. The world of research and policy-making is inextricably linked but is demonstrably different; like the relationship between government and Parliament they operate at a different pace, are influenced by different factors, work using different methods, and have different objectives and priorities. The way in which the two worlds seek to interact needs to reflect this to a much greater degree than at present, and that requires a longer-term strategic approach to policy and legislative development rather than the more *ad hoc*, bill-to-bill approach to consultation that currently characterises too much of the relationship between government and its interface with expertise either through individual researchers or professional bodies.

---

[168] Banking Act 2009, section 10.

Chapter 3: Drafting, access to and quality of the statute book

The drafting of law, translating policy intentions into the formal construct of a bill, is a crucial part of legislative development and the effectiveness of the drafting process is a significant determining factor in the quality of the resulting bill and consequently its passage through the parliamentary scrutiny process. Once the government's policy aims are established, Parliamentary Counsel must shape the legal changes required to achieve them in relation to the law as it currently stands and in such a way that it is comprehensible, accurate, effective and efficient.

The drafting process raises many questions and challenges in the context of making better law. Who is the audience for whom the law is drafted and how does this affect the draft, if at all? How can one balance objectives such as clarity and simplicity of drafting on the one hand with the need to explain what are often highly complex, technical areas of policy on the other? Is it better for the law to be flexible, allowing room for some interpretation by the courts, or does law that conveys particularity better accomplish government objectives? When drafting contemporary law that amends other legislation of long-standing, should the new draft respect current language use or be consistent with the language of the original text? And finally, drafting of primary legislation is placed in the hands of Parliamentary Counsel who are expert in the drafting of law but not in the policy that the law they are drafting is intended to convey. So to what extent, if any, would support and advice from policy and legal experts, particularly in highly complex, technical areas of law, aid drafters in their work?

Although our legal system adheres to the view that ignorance of the law is no defence, much of our law is, in reality, impenetrable to most members of the public. There is nothing novel in this view. As long ago as the 16th century, a young King Edward VI was moved to urge 'that the superfluous and tedious statutes were brought into one sum together, and made plain and short, to the intent that men might better understand them'.[169] Just six years after the Office

---

[169] Report of a Committee Appointed by the Lord President of the Council (May 1975), *The Preparation of Legislation*, Cm 6033, para.2.8, p.6.

of the Parliamentary Counsel was first founded in 1869, a select committee of the House of Commons recommended the consolidation of law and the introduction of the 1889 Interpretation Act to address the legislative problems facing Parliament. And in the 1970s, the Lord President of the Council appointed Sir David Renton to chair a committee composed largely of fellow lawyers to look at the preparation of legislation and how 'greater simplicity and clarity in statute law' might be achieved. [170] But since the 1970s, the volume and complexity of law has grown, exacerbating the difficulties and concerns still further. This chapter explores these challenges in contemporary context. It analyses the strengths and weaknesses of the current drafting system, examines how specialist knowledge might be deployed to strengthen the drafting process, details how improvements might be made to enhance the quality, clarity and integrity of the statute book, as well as expert and public access to it, and considers a number of models for reform of the way in which legislation is written today.

As a lawyer argued in the Hansard Society's publication, *Parliament, Politics and Law Making*, 'Too much legislation is still difficult to follow, hard to find and frustrating to apply, even for lawyers. Legislation does not need to present such problems, which result in much wasted time and money and possibly protracted uncertainty for lawyers and clients alike.' [171] It is these problems that this chapter seeks to address.

Parliamentary Counsel and the drafting process

Despite their importance in the legislative process – performing the critical function of translating the government's policy programme into legislation – there have been relatively few studies, particularly from outside the narrow confines of the academic legal community, of the role and work of the Office of Parliamentary Counsel (OPC). A unit of the Cabinet Office, the day-to-day work of the OPC is actually shaped primarily by the demands of the Cabinet Parliamentary Business and Legislation Committee (PB Committee), its chair the Leader of the House of Commons, and the government's other business managers, namely the Leader of the House of Lords and the Chief Whip in each House.

---

[170] *Ibid.*, para.1.1, p.1.

[171] V. Knapp, 'Law in Practice' in A. Brazier (ed) (2004), *Parliament, Politics and Law Making: Issues and Developments in the Legislative Process* (London: Hansard Society), pp.107-108.

It takes approximately seven years to train Parliamentary Counsel and as of May 2010 the full complement of staff was 82, 60 of whom are legally qualified Counsel with another 22 additional support staff. [172] Throughout the 1990s, the Office never had more than 40 drafters leading Robin Cook, on becoming Leader of the House in 2001, to conclude within a year that despite Counsel's 'positively Stakhanovite commitment to their job', the lack of capacity in the OPC office was 'the real bottleneck on government legislation'. [173] Plans were therefore put in place to substantially increase the number of drafters and consequently their number rose from 40 in 2000 to 60 in 2007. However, although there are now more drafters than a decade ago, in practice only about 80% of the Counsel staff are ever available at any one time for work on government bills, draft bills and SIs as some Counsel are on loan to the Law Commission to help with its work on law reform and one Counsel is lent to the Welsh Assembly Government for two days per week. [174] Given the dramatic increase in the volume of legislation described in chapter 1, this welcome increase in resources can be seen as little more than a belated recognition of the strains placed on the system.

If a government department successfully bids for a bill to be included in the legislative programme, a departmental bill team will be established to shepherd it though all stages of the process from policy to law. The team will consist of a mix of policy officials who advise ministers on the policy being implemented, bill officials who will manage the planning, administration and implementation of the project, and departmental lawyers who will provide legal advice throughout the process to their fellow team members and who are also responsible for producing the drafting instructions for Parliamentary Counsel. A drafting team is also established in the Office of the Parliamentary Counsel to prepare the bill from departmental instructions, advise on any procedural and technical issues and, following introduction in Parliament, to draft any procedural motions or amendments required by the government. The relationship between Parliamentary Counsel and departments is reflected in the Cabinet Office compact, 'Working with Parliamentary Counsel'. [175]

---

[172] Office of the Parliamentary Counsel, 'Working with Parliamentary Counsel', 28 May 2010, pp.6-7, www.cabinetoffice.gov.uk/media/228366/wwpc%2028%20may%202010.pdf.

[173] R. Cook (2003), *The Point of Departure* (London: Simon & Schuster), pp.210-211.

[174] Office of the Parliamentary Counsel, 'Working with Parliamentary Counsel', 28 May 2010, pp.6-7, www.cabinetoffice.gov.uk/media/228366/wwpc%2028%20may%202010.pdf.

[175] *Ibid.*

The role of Parliamentary Counsel is widely considered to centre on two key functions: analysis of ideas and drafting itself. In the view of the former First Parliamentary Counsel, Geoffrey Bowman, 'The drafter's main and most valuable function is to subject policy ideas to rigorous intellectual analysis... It has to stand up to scrutiny in Parliament and (once enacted) to scrutiny by practitioners and the courts.' [176] Depending on the bill, it is not unusual for Parliamentary Counsel to be involved in the planning associated with the legislative project prior to receiving official drafting instructions, particularly if the bill concerns outcomes of a primarily legal character such as a constitutional measure. As First Parliamentary Counsel, Stephen Laws stresses, 'As well as producing the legislative text the Parliamentary Counsel have the function of being guides to the instructing departments through the process of legislating. They are not just wordsmiths: they are also counsel who advise the instructing department on a whole range of matters, including some that may be intimately intertwined with the process of policy formulation.' [177] Experienced drafters can 'alert the department to common traps in the handling of the project and generally volunteer to provide informal and sometimes formal training on bill work'. [178] Parliamentary Counsel come to the policy 'fresh' and with an independent eye and can therefore help uncover any holes in proposals as the whole of the legal framework of the policy is considered. [179] Again, in Bowman's words, the process of legislative drafting 'needs someone who will stand back; who will ruthlessly analyse the ideas; who will question everything with a view to producing something that stands up to scrutiny in Parliament and in the courts; who will break concepts down to their essential components; and who will then express them in easily digestible provisions and in language that is unambiguous, clear and simple'. [180]

The nature of drafting is often piecemeal and instructions from the departmental bill team are usually received in instalments. Drafting instructions are prepared for Parliamentary Counsel by the bill's legal team on the basis of policy instructions.

---

[176] G. Bowman, 'Why is there a Parliamentary Counsel Office?', *Statute Law Review*, 25(69), June 2005, p.70.

[177] S. Laws, 'Drawing the Line', in C. Stefanou & H. Xanthaki (2008), *Drafting legislation: a modern approach* (London: Ashgate), p.20.

[178] S. Laws, 'The Role of Legislative Counsel: Wordsmith or Counsel?', *The Loophole*, (2), August 2008.

[179] A. Graham, 'Well in on the Act – A Government lawyer's view on legislation', *Statute Law Review*, 9(1), Spring 1988, p.12.

[180] G. Bowman, 'Why is there a Parliamentary Counsel Office?', *Statute Law Review*, 25(69), June 2005, p.81.

Good instructions – a 'pearl beyond price' [181] – should set out the factual and political context in which legislation is proposed; the general purpose of the changes proposed; and the principal reasons for legislating. They should convey the existing legal situation and its application in practice, a description of the respects in which, and the extent to which, the existing law prevents the implementation of the department's policy (the 'mischief') and a description of the legal changes to which the bill will give effect in order to provide a remedy for that 'mischief'.

As First Parliamentary Counsel, Stephen Laws, explained at our seminar on drafting, 'instructions in the form of a draft' are not welcomed by drafters as these do not properly convey what the bill seeks to achieve. Without the policy context and an understanding of the 'mischief' and the 'remedy', the drafting team have no way of knowing whether the draft has achieved what was intended. Drafting instructions, in contrast, provide an explanation of the bill's intended outcomes against which the draft can be tested.

Once a draft has been written it will be circulated to relevant officials within the department for comment and consideration. Depending on the time available it may also be circulated more widely among stakeholders particularly with any other body that may have a role in implementing the legislation, such as a regulator. If the bill is subject to pre-legislative scrutiny then this is regarded as a further round of drafting with extended deadlines for consultation purposes.

Each bill and drafting team, through an exchange of drafts, seek to test out the basis for legislation and the efficacy of the draft. Is the premise for the proposed legal change correct and complete? Are there any other legal obstacles to be overcome? Is the 'mischief' accurately described: how is the remedy to be framed and what degree of precision is required? Will the remedy provide the result being sought? Have related issues such as trans-national provisions, territorial application in the context of devolution, and issues concerning the use and disclosure of data all been dealt with as necessary in the draft? And is the draft compatible with the Human Rights Act 1998?

Drafting quality

The quality of the draft presented to Parliament is directly linked to the quality of the future Act. Without a good draft, there is the potential for a range of

---

[181] G.C. Thornton (1996), *Legislative Drafting* (London: Butterworths), p.127.

damaging consequences, from excessive amendments, particularly of a technical nature, during the passage of the bill to 'fix' problems in the draft, to hastily enacted provisions that simply do not work. Indeed, it is far from unusual for government to table hundreds of amendments to a bill as it progresses through Parliament. The implications of this may then be felt in both Houses of Parliament as the time of both MPs and peers is spent addressing drafting pitfalls to the exclusion of other issues, thereby potentially overlooking other unforeseen consequences in the legislation on which they might otherwise have concentrated. A poorly prepared, 'half-baked' draft also risks embarrassing the bill minister and business managers, and causing knock-on delays in the passage of other legislation. [182]

Parliamentary Counsel are often criticised directly and indirectly, and particularly by legislators, for the quality of legislative drafting today. They are blamed for the prolix nature of Acts, for legislation that appears to replicate existing offences, and for the impenetrable nature of some bills. But such criticism fails to take account of both the enormously complex challenges that drafters face in turning policy into law, and the external pressures over which they often have very limited control, most notably the volume of legislation, the limited resources at their disposal, and the time constraints imposed by ministers on the preparation of bills. The quality of their draft can only ever be as clear as the policy that shapes it and if there is internal disagreement within government this can also cause huge problems affecting the direction of the draft in terms of either its complexity or its simplicity. Taken together, these factors all have a detrimental impact on their work.

But constraints on time for effective preparation of both drafting instructions and the draft itself have perhaps the most regularly significant impact on the quality of the final product. As the Office of the Parliamentary Counsel itself notes, 'The conditions for preparing instructions are seldom ideal, and it is not unusual for compromises to have to be made to cope with the pressures of the timetable, or a delay in decision-making.' [183] On occasion these can border on the comical, as in the case of the drafting of the Dangerous Dogs Act 1991 which was produced in haste, and amidst much political and media pressure,

---

[182] Office of the Parliamentary Counsel, 'Working with Parliamentary Counsel', 28 May 2010, p.26, www.cabinetoffice.gov.uk/media/228366/wwpc%2028%20may%202010.pdf.

[183] *Ibid.*

following a spate of dog attacks on children. As it was later reported, '…the story doing the rounds in Westminster at the time was that Parliamentary Counsel had said they couldn't define a Pit-Bull Terrier and the Home Secretary replied "well you could if you had one hanging on your elbow" and the legislation therefore contains the definition "a Pit-Bull Terrier is a dog of the kind commonly known as a Pit-Bull Terrier".' [184]

The knock-on effects of time pressures are keenly felt during the parliamentary stages of the legislative process, as was seen during the passage of the Legislative and Regulatory Reform Bill in 2006. Here, the government sought to replace the Regulatory Reform Orders for removing administrative burdens on business as originally established in the Regulatory Reform Act 2001. The procedure was deemed by departments to be overly demanding and time-consuming, and had been subject to wide criticism for its under-utilisation. [185] Following a public consultation lasting from July to October 2005, a bill was rushed to Parliament for first reading on 11 January 2006. The devising of a new procedure for the removal of administrative burdens was clearly a complex one, and two months was far from sufficient to achieve it. The bill was the subject of considerable criticism for the inclusion of wide-ranging Henry VIII powers for ministers that went well beyond the scope of the policy proposed in the original consultation. Reflecting on the bill, a departmental official referred to it as a 'work in progress' and asserted that there had been pressure from ministers to get a bill before Parliament that had resulted in a rushed job. [186] The scale of the discontent in Parliament prompted the government to move five new clauses and 74 amendments at report stage in the House of Commons.

Beyond internally imposed pressures, Parliamentary Counsel must also tackle externally focused challenges, the first of which is that when drafting they must have an eye to several different audiences, the needs and interests of which can be difficult to balance. In theory, the audience to whom the technical quality and effectiveness of any bill is directed above all is the courts – in that it must be robust enough to withstand judicial challenge. In practical terms

---

[184] BBC Radio 4, *The Draftsman's Contract*, broadcast 17 December 2008, Jonathan Bracken cited in transcript at p.2, http://www.cabinetoffice.gov.uk/media/210695/draftsmanscontract2.pdf.

[185] A. Brazier, S. Kalitowski & G. Rosenblatt with M. Korris (2008), *Law in the Making: Influence and Change in the Legislative Process* (London: Hansard Society), pp.101-102.

[186] *Ibid.*, p.121.

however, a bill must also consider the needs of legislators for it must be capable of being passed in Parliament. As former Parliamentary Counsel Daniel Greenberg writes, 'Parliament is our primary client and the courts are our "ultimate" client.' [187] But it has also long been accepted that law should be accessible to citizens whose affairs may be concerned in the legislation, not least in order to foster compliance with its demands. As Greenberg summarises, responsibility lies with the drafter to ensure that 'the law is drafted in such a way as to make its effect accessible to all those readers who could reasonably require to understand it'. [188] Sometimes this audience will be ordinary citizens; at other times it may be a more discrete section of the public. Inevitably then, given the range of audiences, it is difficult to satisfy the needs and interests of everyone. The 1975 Renton Report recommended that the interests of the 'ultimate user' should always have priority over legislators and this now governs the approach of the OPC. [189]

The second challenge lies in deciding what to include and what to omit in the draft. As former First Parliamentary Counsel, Geoffrey Bowman contends, 'Excluding the wrong material from the legislative text is just as important as including the right material in it. Legislation has a very precise object. And that is to change the law – no more and no less. Every word counts and every proposition will be assumed to have a purpose. If you include unnecessary material you are inviting trouble. As a Parliamentary Counsel once said, "Excess matter in bills, as in people, tends to go septic".' [190]

Here the drafter faces tensions between competing desires: in the interests of greater certainty the bill should aspire to as much clarity as possible but this may result in a more complex, long-winded bill; on the other hand if the drafters look to greater simplicity they may reduce the complexity but also the certainty and clarity of the bill's intent. 'The expertise of the drafter is often called on to set the parameters for any discretion', explains Stephen

---

[187] D. Greenberg, 'The nature of legislative intention and its implications for legislative drafting', *Statute Law Review*, 27(1), 2006, pp.15-28.

[188] D. Greenberg (2009), *Access to legislation – the drafter's role*, section 4, www.cabinetoffice.gov.uk/media/274184/access.to.legislation.01.pdf.

[189] Report of a Committee Appointed by the Lord President of the Council (May 1975), *The Preparation of Legislation*, Cm 6033, para10.3, p.56.

[190] G. Bowman, 'Why is there a Parliamentary Counsel Office?', *Statute Law Review*, 26(69), June 2005, p.77.

Laws. 'In doing that the drafter has to decide to what extent those parameters need to be tightly drawn in order to secure that the discretion will be exercised in the manner intended.' [191] However, rather than an emphasis on discretion, overly-detailed legislation – or particularism – is regarded as a growing problem, with bills being produced that seek to provide for every eventuality. As Jeremy Horder, then Professor of Criminal Law at the Law Commission, explained at our seminar, reliance on more general prohibitions governing the same issues 'would mean less law, and in all probability more consistency'. [192] He pointed to the infamous 'goldfish in a bag' case in section 11 of the Animal Welfare Act 2006 that set out in detail an offence that in essence criminalised the sale of animals, including as a prize, to those under the age of 16, with a potential punishment of imprisonment for up to 51 weeks attached to it. Thus, the 'goldfish in a bag won by a child at a school fete', became a legislative *cause celebre.*

The 'goldfish in a bag' case study

Section 11 of the Animal Welfare Act 2006 reads:

'(3) A person commits an offence if –

(a) he enters into an arrangement with a person whom he has reasonable cause to believe to be under the age of 16 years, and

(b) the arrangement is one under which that person has the chance to win an animal as a prize.

(4) A person does not commit an offence under subsection (3) if –

(a) he enters into the arrangement in the presence of the person with whom the arrangement is made, and

(b) he has reasonable cause to believe that the person with whom the arrangement is made is accompanied by a person who is not under the age of 16 years.

(5) A person does not commit an offence under subsection (3) if –

(a) he enters into the arrangement otherwise than in the presence of

---

[191] S. Laws, 'Drawing the Line', in C. Stefanou & H. Xanthaki (2008), *Drafting legislation: a modern approach* (London: Ashgate), p.29.

[192] J. Horder, 'Drafting (Criminal) Laws', unpublished paper for the Hansard Society Making Better Law seminar, July 2009, p.3.

      the person with whom the arrangement is made, and

  (b) he has reasonable cause to believe that a person who has actual care and control of the person with whom the arrangement is made has consented to the arrangement.

  (6) A person does not commit an offence under subsection (3) if he enters into the arrangement in a family context.' [193]

The drafting of this part of the Act was widely derided at our seminar as being littered with 'ifs' and 'buts', and rendered overly complicated. It was argued that a later part of the Act, the offence set out in section 9(1) would have sufficed, namely: 'A person commits an offence if he does not take such steps as are reasonable in all the circumstances to ensure that the needs of an animal for which he is responsible are met to the extent required by good practice.' [194]

As Jeremy Horder set out at our seminar, 'you might think that what section 11(3) prohibits is in principle covered by section 9. This is because selling a goldfish in a bag (say) to an unaccompanied 15-year-old is a failure to take reasonable steps, when the animal is handed over, to ensure its needs are met, for the purposes of section 9. And if that is right, when a fairground operator sells a goldfish to an unaccompanied child, why not just charge section 9? To be sure, that will mean not every instance of goldfish-selling to children will be found criminal, but then section 11 already anticipates that some such sales are OK. And section 9 is sensitive to 'good practice' development, which could expressly deal with the goldfish problem. Even if that is a bit speculative, would not a bit of speculation have been worth it? The real object is law simply expressed.' [195]

---

[193] Animal Welfare Act 2006, section 11.

[194] *Ibid.*, section 9(1).

[195] J. Horder, 'Drafting (Criminal) Laws', unpublished paper for the Hansard Society Making Better Law seminar, July 2009, p. 3. He noted additionally that 'the policy to be implemented through section 11(3) is unclear. Nowhere is it stated that the person to whom the prize is given (the receiver) must actually be under 16 at the relevant time. It is enough that the provider has reasonable cause to believe that the receiver is under 16. If the underlying policy is to punish wicked fairground operators, then there is indeed no policy requirement that the receiver in fact be under 16. However, if the policy is in part to protect animals from children's well-known tendency to forget about animal welfare when a pet is a couple of months old, then the courts perhaps ought to imply a requirement that the receiver actually be under 16.'

The more the drafter seeks to draft exhaustively the more there is the possibility of loopholes and therefore the greater the possibility of potential challenges. It also has the effect of lengthening the statute book. On the other hand, there are occasions when greater detail may be necessary: for example, in relation to the implementation of aspects of European law. And, as Horder again argues, not all specificity is wrong: there are good reasons, for example, for a separate crime of 'rape' rather than subsuming this in a general crime of violence. [196] But critics of the detailed length of legislation are equally wary of judicial interpretation of statutes that may result from less detailed Acts where judges have to make fine legal interpretations and distinctions. As Stephen Laws notes, in the final analysis, 'The question of how much detail should be inserted in a legislative provision and how much should be left to a discretion to be operated in practice is primarily a question of policy for those who instruct the drafter.' [197] As the Renton Committee found in 1975, 'the draftsman must never be forced to sacrifice certainty for simplicity, since the result may be to frustrate the legislative intention. An unfortunate subject may be driven to litigation because the meaning of an Act was obscure which could, by the use of a few extra words, have been made plain.' [198] But the decision on the fine balance to be struck between restrictive or permissive drafting is ultimately a political decision that lies with government, though it is clearly an area where drafters should and do have a voice in the internal debate.

The importance of this debate extends not just to the body of a bill but also to its titles. Parliamentary Counsel give each bill drafted both a short and a long title. [199] The short title is the name that the bill and subsequent Act will be known as, while the long title must encompass the whole content of the bill. The short title is usually three to seven words long, but depending on the range of subjects covered by the bill and how detailed the provisions are, the long title can vary from one to several clauses in length. As the bill evolves before

---

[196] J. Horder, 'Rethinking non-Fatal Offences Against the Person', *Oxford Journal of Legal Studies*, 14(3), 1994, p.340.

[197] S. Laws, 'Drawing the Line', in C. Stefanou & H. Xanthaki (eds) (2008), *Draft Legislation: a modern approach* (London: Ashgate), p.29.

[198] Report of a Committee Appointed by the Lord President of the Council (May 1975), *The Preparation of Legislation*, Cm 6033, para11.5, p.62.

[199] Cabinet Office, *Guide to making Legislation*, para.9.31, http://www.cabinetoffice.gov.uk/making-legislation-guide/drafting_the_bill.aspx.

introduction there is a pressure to delay drafting the long title in case policy changes and new clauses are needed, as the long title must reflect all the content of the bill. It is drafted precisely in order to avoid restricting the scope for additional provisions to be added to the bill.[200] Parliament can amend both the short and long titles of a bill during the scrutiny process but this is relatively rare; government usually resists any attempt to broaden the scope or change the focus of its legislation.

Drafting and expertise

In the last analysis the OPC has an obligation not just to the government but also to the maintenance of the integrity of the statute book. They retain a powerful hand in any negotiations with ministers and officials over the draft of a bill because they have the right to refer their concerns to the Attorney General if they believe that their drafting instructions put them in conflict with this duty to the statute book. But the extent to which the OPC acts as a restraint on government in terms of influencing the making of better law is difficult to determine. Firstly, as lawyers, what passes between Counsel and government departments remains confidential and therefore evidence rather than anecdote is hard to come by. But as Page found in a recent study of the impact of Parliamentary Counsel on policy analysis, drafters are 'quite stoical that politicians must be given what they want', even 'where the need for new legislation, or at least legislation with wide scope, is doubted', although they will 'seek to stop departments bringing unnecessary "spin" into the wording of the legislation and also the explanatory material'.[201] Parliamentary Counsel can advise ministers and officials about how powers are defined and raise questions and concerns about consistency of provisions in different legislative measures but as civil servants they adhere to the principles of political neutrality – it is for ministers, not Counsel, to decide whether to press ahead with legislation. Having done so, it is for the drafter to give effect to the government's wishes in the clearest manner possible.

This may be the right position in terms of our parliamentary system and the independent neutrality of the civil service. However, it is difficult to ignore the

---

[200] D. Greenberg (ed) (2008), *Craies on Legislation*, 9th Edition (London: Sweet & Maxwell) at footnote 101 and associated text.

[201] E.C. Page, 'Their word is law: parliamentary counsel and creative analysis policy', *Public Law*, October 2009, pp.790-811.

siren voices of concern about the current state of the statute book, many of them heard at our seminars. **In light of these concerns the time has come to reassess the scope for providing some oversight (at least of a light touch nature) of the work of the OPC through the deployment of external expertise and support on either a permanent or *ad hoc* basis.**

As Page found, 'A drafting monopoly held by a small group of officials, such as found in the United Kingdom is not a common arrangement', although it is certainly a characteristic of Westminster-model parliamentary systems. [202] However, Parliamentary Counsel are not the only legislative drafters at Westminster. Departmental lawyers draft delegated legislation, Private Bills are drafted by Parliamentary Agents who are usually based with legal firms specialising in such legislation, and Private Members' Bills (PMBs) are generally drafted either by the MP or peer sponsoring the bill with the advice of Parliament's Public Bill Office, or by a supportive external organisation (although Parliamentary Counsel do draft 'handout bills' for government departments to pass to backbenchers to champion).

There has been some limited experimentation with utilising external drafters in the past but the results have been decidedly mixed. In 1996, private practitioners were brought in to draft part of the Finance Bill (nine clauses and three schedules) but as Daintith and Page concluded, 'As well as being very expensive the contractors' work was thought to be opaque and "over-drafted".' [203] MPs were no less critical. Ian Pearson MP commented, 'At 408 pages long, the bill represents a 15% rise in output from the combined talents of the parliamentary and private sector drafting staff compared with the previous year. It has a third more clauses, adding to the 1,500 pages of primary tax legislation already introduced in the past five years.' [204] In the view of his parliamentary colleague, Tim Smith, there was 'no evidence' that the private sector practitioners had been able to improve on the work of the Office of the Parliamentary Counsel. [205] 'It was not a success', noted Geoffrey Bowman, and 'has not been repeated.' [206]

---

[202] *Ibid.*

[203] T. Daintith & A. Page (1999), *The Executive and the Constitution* (Oxford: Oxford University Press), p.251.

[204] Ian Pearson MP, *Hansard*, 15 January 1996, vol. 269 col. 460.

[205] Tim Smith MP, *Hansard*, 15 January 1996, vol. 269 col. 425.

[206] G. Bowman, 'Why is there a Parliamentary Counsel Office?', *Statute Law Review*, 25(69), June 2005, p.81.

Internationally, there are examples where expert assistance is provided to drafters but on the basis of providing support not control, and usually with regard to improving the language and simplicity of bills. In New Zealand, for example, there are editorial staff who 'proof read and provide quality assurance for legislation during the drafting and publishing processes'. [207]

Proponents of the current system argue that as drafters work as a team there is already an element of peer review in the drafting process and an internal Drafting Techniques Group produces recommendations and papers from time to time on particular drafting issues. [208] Drafters are also able to seek information from the department instructing them on any matters requiring expertise. Critics of external support argue that it will build in an extra process through which legislation has to pass and will therefore simply exacerbate the existing strains on time and resources.

In a new initiative the Office of the Parliamentary Counsel requested and secured the inclusion of questions on technical drafting issues as part of the consultation on the draft Flooding and Water Management Bill in 2009. [209] It sought the public's views on 'presentation structure and other drafting issues', including whether the legislation was written 'in a reasonably clear style that is likely to be understood by readers'; whether the individual clauses and sentences were too long, too short, or about the right length; and whether there were drafting techniques people would like to see used more or less. The response of the Environment Select Committee was not positive, describing the bill as a 'confusing mix of measures, many of them poorly drafted'. [210] **This initiative would need to be repeated, across a range of draft bills, to ascertain whether it adds value to the drafting process but if so it could be a useful vehicle for greater expert input at this stage of legislative development as part of wider improvements to government consultation processes. To this end then, the Office of the Parliamentary Counsel might seek agreement on a protocol with government departments whereby**

---

[207] Parliamentary Counsel Office, New Zealand, http://www.pco.parliament.govt.nz/law-drafting.

[208] Office of the Parliamentary Counsel (October 2010), *Drafting Guidance*, http://www.cabinetoffice.gov.uk/media/427772/drafting-guidance-101002.pdf.

[209] Department for Environment, Food and Rural Affairs (April 2009), *Draft Flood and Water Management Bill*, Cm 7582, p.22.

[210] House of Commons Environment, Food and Rural Affairs Committee (2008-09), *The Draft Flood and Water Management Bill*, HC 555, p.3.

technical issues, such as those explored in the Flood and Water Management bill draft, are included in all future draft bill consultation documents. If undertaken, there should then be a full and open assessment and evaluation of its effectiveness.

Another option for engaging external expertise and some light-touch oversight of the drafting process would be via a Legislative Draft Readers' Panel of experts drawn to reflect the intended audience of the bill, including judges, and perhaps drawing on a broad body of professions, particularly in highly technical policy areas, to include people with a background in science, medicine, business, technology, social security, the environment and so on. Here, a small group of specialists with front-line knowledge of how certain words and phrases are interpreted and utilised in key areas, particularly of criminal law, might help the drafting process by considering a draft prior to its formalisation as a bill. Their role would an advisory one; they would possess no powers to instruct Parliamentary Counsel to implement any drafting changes. However, with their experience of dealing with the legislation once enacted, their viewpoint could be of particular assistance in considering practical consequences and 'usability' of proposals as well as stimulating informed debate about the technical elements of the draft.

The Hansard Society's Rippon Commission on the Legislative Process considered the introduction of an expert panel in 1993. [211] It envisaged an independent or quasi-independent body consisting of judges, other lawyers and lay people, with a remit to consider constitutional, legal and other non-policy matters. The Commission eventually declined to support the proposal for three reasons: the system of a single drafting office means there is less need for oversight; any panel would have to include legislative drafters (rather than just judges or other lawyers), and such scrutiny would take extra time. The latter argument remains compelling, perhaps even more so today given the time pressures in the legislative system. However, the other arguments are much less convincing. It should be possible to include drafters on the Panel, and if not then other drafters from a Westminster-style parliamentary system might be approached. And whilst a single drafting office has advantages in terms of uniformity and consistency it can also have disadvantages in terms of narrowness of thinking. On balance, given the criticisms of legislation today, we

---

[211] Hansard Society (1993), *Making the Law: the report of the Hansard Society Commission on the Legislative Process* (London: Hansard Society), paras 190-198.

think **there is merit in establishing a Legislative Draft Readers' Panel on a trial basis in this Parliament.**

Acknowledging that government legislation is 'often hastily drafted, leading to unintended consequences in the law', the Conservative Party prior to the general election outlined plans to pilot a new 'crowd-sourcing' approach to the drafting of legislation to enable 'expert' members of the public, particularly academics and lawyers, to play a role in the process and thus, they hoped, help produce better bills. [212] The pilot they outlined consisted of four stages. First the department sponsoring the legislation would publish detailed instructions on the policy intentions of the legislation online, as well as an explanation of the constraints within which all clauses would have to be drafted. Interested members of the public would then register for an online forum that would allow them to submit draft clauses they believed would achieve the specified policy aims. The third stage would see all the public contributions opened to review, comment and amendment from other registered participants utilising some form of ratings system. Finally, at the end of the process, the highest rated drafts would be sent for consideration by the OPC. The decision as to whether or not to accept any of the top rated drafting suggestions would be a matter solely for the OPC. The initial plan was to pilot this innovation with one bill during the first legislative session, complementing the party's plans for an online public reading stage. Although plans are underway to establish this legislative stage, the proposal for a public drafting process appears to have been delayed, if not dropped. Given the problems with the drafting process however, and particularly the wide criticism it evokes among lawyers and academics, it would be an interesting project to test on at least one bill to see if there genuinely are any advantages to be gained from it. **We therefore recommend that the government pilot a crowd-source public drafting project on one bill in this Parliament.**

Legal interpretation: *Pepper v Hart*

A factor that a number of attendees at our seminars feared may be inhibiting our ability to make better law is the difficulties posed by the *Pepper*

---

[212] Conservative Party, *'Big Ideas To Give Britain Real Change'*, 24 April 2010, p.7. The concept was based in part on a 2007 pilot project, 'Peer to Patent' run by the United States' Patent and Trademark Office.

(Inspector of Taxes) v Hart legal ruling in 1993. [213] As a result of this House of Lords decision, if primary legislation is deemed 'ambiguous' or 'obscure' the courts may take account of statements in Parliament by ministers when interpreting the law. [214] Hitherto, the courts had never used *Hansard* as an aid to statute interpretation as this was deemed to breach parliamentary privilege under article 9 of the 1689 Bill of Rights. As the Joint Committee on Parliamentary Privilege described it, 'The House of Lords in its judicial capacity decided that clear statements made in Parliament concerning the purpose of legislation in course of enactment may be used by the court as a guide to the interpretation of ambiguous statutory provisions. The Lords held such use of statements did not infringe article 9 because it did not amount to questioning a proceeding in Parliament. Far from questioning the independence of Parliament and its debates, the courts would be giving effect to what was said and done there.' [215]

The applicability of the *Pepper v Hart* ruling was laid out by Lord Browne-Wilkinson who set three tests to determine whether *Hansard* could be used to aid interpretation, namely where:

- the words of the statute are ambiguous, obscure or the literal interpretation leads to an absurdity;

- the material consists of statement(s) by a minister or promoter of the bill, together with material necessary to understand the statements and;

- the statement is clear. [216]

There were certainly efforts in the courts, in the early years after the case, to use the doctrine more freely than these tests would support, but the primary concern is the extent to which the judgement may be inhibiting Parliament from free debate. Some attendees at our seminar attested strongly that the implications of the case were destroying the quality of legislative debate as ministers were worried about how any comments and commitments uttered during the course of debate might subsequently be interpreted by the judiciary. As one seminar

---

[213] For an account of the case see C. Littleboy & R. Kelly, *'Pepper v Hart'*, House of Commons Library Standard Note, SN/PC/392, 22 June 2005.

[214] Lord Browne-Wilkinson *Pepper v Hart* [1993] AC 593 at 634.

[215] *Ibid.*

[216] *Ibid.*, at 640.

participant noted, reliance on ministerial statements carries dangers as these are often made at short notice and are heavy on political posturing and point-scoring, and government ministers, either ill-briefed or over-enthusiastic in their approach, may give assurances that go beyond what the legislation will allow in instances where there is some ambiguity.

Many commenting on the use of *Hansard* note that it will rarely provide a definitive statement on the point at issue. As Lord Reid has argued, 'we would be looking for a needle in a haystack and more often than not the needle is not there'. [217] Concerns have also been expressed that private assurances to MPs and peers, often given in correspondence, now, as a direct result of this case, need to be placed on the record. Hence, in July 2009, during debate on the Parliamentary Standards Bill, Lord Higgins read out an extract from a letter he had received from the Leader of the House, thus ensuring it was recorded in *Hansard*, in case the matter ever came before the courts. [218]

An alternative view is put by Kavanagh who asserts that as a result of the case, government, rather than shrinking from commitments in debate, has actively sought to steer debate in a particular direction with an eye to influencing subsequent judicial interpretation: 'It is certainly the case that since *Pepper v Hart* many statements have been made in parliamentary debates with the possibility of litigation in mind.' [219] One seminar participant indicated that bill teams have been known to script ministerial responses to key questions specifically to ensure that exactly the right words appear on the record.

There is an on-going debate about whether the impact of the doctrine will also be felt in the long-term at the drafting level. If there is less pressure to provide certainty by covering all conceivable eventualities because ministerial statements can buttress the legislation, then this might point to the utilisation of simpler legislative drafting techniques in the future. [220] However, as Edward Leigh MP noted in debate on the Gender Recognition Bill in 2004, 'Surely we cannot and must not come to the stage at which ministers refer to *Pepper v Hart* in advance of a bill becoming an Act, saying, "Don't worry, the bill does

---

[217] Lord Reid (1972-73), 'The Judge as Law-Maker', 12 JSPTL 22 at 28, cited in S. Vogenauer (2005), 'A Retreat from *Pepper v Hart*? A reply to Lord Steyn', *Oxford Journal of Legal Studies*, 25(4), p.631.

[218] Lord Higgins, *Hansard*, 16 July 2009, vol. 712 col. 1298.

[219] A. Kavanagh, '*Pepper v Hart*: Matters of constitutional principle', *Law Quarterly Review*, 120, 2005, p.107.

[220] J. Jenkins (1994), '*Pepper v Hart*: A Draftsman's Perspective', *Statute Law Review*, 15(1), p.24.

not need to be entirely clear. I am now giving a *Pepper v Hart* statement. Lawyers in future can refer back to my remarks, so what I am saying should give reassurance"...... Should we not try to make the legislation watertight before we reach that stage?' [221]

Some legal experts contend that the difficulties of *Pepper v Hart* are exaggerated as the courts have made clear that they recognise the case in *contra proferentem,* a legal rule that an ambiguity in a document is construed against the party who drafted it. In the case of legislation the contract party (the government) is therefore encouraged to be as clear as possible in their contract, namely the Act of Parliament. Several seminar participants suggested that this meant that the right way to get something on the record was, as ever, through probing amendments, rather than statements in some other form.

Whatever the truth of the legal situation, it is clear that some have serious concerns and as yet there is no definitive and settled view on the impact of the doctrine.

Understanding and accessing legislation

That legislation should be accessible, intelligible and clear to all audiences is both a democratic right and also an essential prerequisite in the process of making better law. For parliamentarians and external expert stakeholders in particular, it is a significant factor in determining the quality of scrutiny that can be brought to legislative proposals and therefore ultimately the quality of the final law that emerges. But as *Law in the Making* noted 'Parliamentarians were often open in admitting that coping with the reality of massive amounts of complicated legislation severely compromised their effectiveness, and that they often do not understand the subject matter of the bills they are scrutinising. This is despite the fact that information supporting the legislative process has been significantly improved.' [222]

Given the complexities and increasing length of legislation, there is a perennial debate about what innovations might be introduced to aid understanding of and access to legislation by a range of different audiences.

---

[221] Edward Leigh MP, *Hansard*, 25 May 2004, vol. 421 col. 1453.

[222] A. Brazier, S. Kalitowski & G. Rosenblatt with M. Korris (2008), *Law in the Making: Influence and Change in the Legislative Process* (London: Hansard Society), p.194.

i) Purpose or overview clauses

Legislators in particular find 'purpose' or 'overview' clauses a useful tool but they have not yet become the norm in drafting. A purpose clause, as the name suggests, sets out the purpose behind a statute. It is contained within the Act itself but is additional to the main provisions and detailed rules. [223] For example: Section 1(1) of the Banking Act 2009 reads: 'The purpose of the special resolution regime for banks is to address the situation where all or part of the business of a bank has encountered, or is likely to encounter, financial difficulties.' [224] While not adding a substantive provision to the Act, this sets the scene, and aids interpretation.

Some drafters are often reluctant to utilise them however, as they can create ambiguity and they can be hard to draft. Geoffrey Bowman claimed never to have drafted one in his career as a Parliamentary Counsel. 'One problem is that it is not always easy to say what the purpose of a bill is', he said. 'As Professor Reed Dickerson said, purpose provisions tend to "degenerate into pious incantations ... such as ... the one in [an] Ecology Bill, which in substance said 'Hurrah for Nature!'" Another problem is that the specific provisions and the purpose provision might conflict. If so, which is to prevail? And even if there is no obvious conflict, the relationship between the specific provisions and the purpose provision may not be clear.' [225]

When the Public Administration Committee considered the draft Freedom of Information Bill in 1999 it recommended a purpose clause in order to set the 'tone and spirit' of the Act. [226] As David Clark MP suggested during the debate on the bill, it would 'get across to the ordinary man and woman in the street that he or she had the right to access'. [227] Greenberg has gone further and suggested that greater use of overview clauses might provide for greater electronic searchability and accessibility of statute law in the future, in effect providing for the data 'tagging' of legislation that would aid broader public

---

[223] G. Bowman, 'Why is there a Parliamentary Counsel Office?', *Statute Law Review*, 25(69), June 2005.

[224] Banking Act 2009, section 1(1).

[225] G. Bowman, 'Why is there a Parliamentary Counsel Office?', *Statute Law Review*, 25(69), June 2005, p.78.

[226] House of Commons Public Administration Committee (1998-99), *Freedom of Information Draft Bill*, para.59.

[227] David Clark MP, *Hansard*, 7 December 1999, vol. 340 col 741.

access to the law. If overview clauses were to become an established component of legislation, he argues, it could 'enable databases to include it in the way they handle and arrange data' and so provide a new and valuable navigational technique for readers. [228] Users of the legislation would then be able to produce, at the touch of a button, 'what would amount in effect to a series of single-sentence summaries of the topics and sub-topics addressed by a piece of legislation, knowing that each sentence was part of the law itself and was therefore determinative and authoritative in a way that explanatory material, however helpful, of its nature is not'. [229]

But the appetite for purpose clauses among backbench legislators has never been matched by ministers as then Solicitor-General Vera Baird's retort to John Mason MP's request for a purpose clause in the 2010 Equality Bill, sums up: 'I do not think that a purpose clause would be a useful tool…. A purpose clause is not part of what we usually do in English statute, and there is no particular reason to put it in here. I do not know whether any statement of purpose would go beyond the full contents of the statute itself to help where there is a conflict between strands.' [230] The resistance of government to purpose clauses is borne out by their infrequent use: of 27 Acts which received Royal Assent in 2009, only three included a purpose clause. [231]

In its 1993 Rippon Commission report *Making the Law* the Hansard Society recommended that statements of principle or purpose should not be adopted as a general practice but left to the drafter's discretion. It saw 'considerable problems in including in an Act two different formulations of what must be intended to be the same law on a single point – one in the form of a statement of principle or purpose (in some cases perhaps both) and the other in the form of detailed provisions'. In many cases, the result would be, it argued, 'a recipe for confusion, with some people relying on one formulation and some on the other'. [232] More recently the House of Lords Constitution Committee

---

[228] D. Greenberg (2009), *Access to legislation – the drafter's role*, pp.6-7, www.cabinetoffice.gov.uk/media/274184/access.to.legislation.01.pdf.

[229] *Ibid.*, p.7.

[230] Vera Baird MP, Equality Bill Committee, 4th Sitting, 9 June 2009, col. 110.

[231] Section 1(2) of the Business Rates Supplements Act 2009; Section 1(1) of the Green Energy (Definition and Promotion) Act 2009; and Section 1(1) of the Banking Act 2009.

[232] Hansard Society (1993), *Making the Law: The report of the Hansard Society Commission on the Legislative Process* (London: Hansard Society), paras 241-242.

recommended that use of purpose clauses be left to the discretion of the drafter, but that a statement of purpose should be included in the explanatory notes to bills. The committee indicated that the statement should include standards against which to measure the Act during post-legislative scrutiny. [233]

Understanding of legislation, in part driven by constraints on accessibility, is a particular problem in terms of public knowledge and understanding of the legislative process in those instances where citizens might wish or need to know more about particular statutes. The consensus is in favour of the employment of purpose clauses at the discretion of Parliamentary Counsel.

An alternative non-legislative approach to making plain the purpose of the provisions of an Act can be found in a 2007 Department of Trade and Industry innovation that could be replicated across government. Following consultation with stakeholders in light of the passage of the 2006 Companies Act, the department published a reference guide for business setting out ministerial statements on the duties of company directors. Referring to the debates on the Act the minister, Margaret Hodge MP, stated in the foreword to the guidance, 'During those debates, I and the other ministers were questioned about the meaning of the provisions. Some of our responses and statements may be helpful to people interested in what the provisions mean, and I am pleased to be publishing this structured collection of what we believe are the most useful of them.' [234] At just 14 pages long, the guidance was clear, accessible and informative, whilst stressing that it should not be regarded as a substitute for reading the Act or seeking legal advice if required. Such a guidance model could readily be rolled out across other legislative areas in order to provide clarity for interested and affected stakeholders but should not excuse ambiguous or poorly-drafted legislation.

ii) Keeling Schedules

If a bill makes substantial changes to an existing Act of Parliament it can be difficult to tell what the amended Act will look like. A valuable aid to scrutiny would therefore be the introduction of 'Keeling Schedules' to bills. [235]

---

[233] House of Lords Constitution Committee (2003-04), *Parliament and the Legislative Process*, HL 173, paras 86-87.

[234] Department of Trade and Industry (June 2007), *Companies Act 2006 – Duties of company directors: ministerial statements*, p.1, www.berr.gov.uk/files/file40139.pdf.

[235] Keeling Schedules are named after Sir Edward Keeling, Conservative MP for Twickenham from 1935 to 1954, who was in the vanguard of parliamentary pressure to make it easier to understand how existing Acts were affected by amendments in a new bill.

The most common way of amending legislation is by reference in a bill indicating where new words should be inserted into the existing Act. While this 'patchwork drafting' achieves the necessary legal effect, it can be very difficult for parliamentarians and outside observers to see what the effect of the change will be. [236] For example, the Academies Act 2010 amended eight existing Acts of Parliament. [237] Schedule 2 of the bill provided that the Education Act 2002 should be amended as follows:

'(12) In section 65 (Academies) omit subsection (2).

(13) Section 67 (conversion of city academies into Academies) is repealed.

(14) Section 68 (city colleges) is repealed.

(15) In Schedule 1 (incorporation and powers of governing bodies) in paragraph 5(2)(a) (dissolution of governing body) omit the "or" after sub-paragraph (ii) and after sub-paragraph (iii) insert ", or

(iv) the date on which a local authority are required to cease to maintain the school under section 6(2) of the Academies Act 2010;".' [238]

Anyone scrutinising the bill needs to have a copy of the existing section of the Act to hand and work out what the differences are, and, if the old Act has been amended by a number of subsequent Acts they will all need to be taken into account by the reader as well. As the House of Lords Constitution Committee noted, 'It is extraordinarily difficult at times to appreciate the effect of a bill on an earlier Act without seeing the Act and how it is amended by the bill. The Explanatory Notes provide some help but they are no substitute for looking at the original measure and seeing how precisely the bill changes it.' [239] Given the frequency of amendment and addition to existing Acts which has been described in chapter 1, this factor can make proposed legislation, and its effects, almost impossible for MPs and peers to understand while it is passing through Parliament.

---

[236] Lord Brightman (2002), 'Drafting Quagmires', *Statute Law Review*, 23(1), May 2002, p.4.

[237] Education Act 1996; School Standards and Framework Act 1998; Education Act 2002 Education Act 2005; Education and Inspections Act 2006; Education and Skills Act 2008; Apprenticeships, Skills, Children and Learning Act 2009; Children, Schools and Families Act 2010.

[238] Academies Act 2010, schedule 2.

[239] House of Lords Constitution Committee (2003-04), *Parliament and the Legislative Process*, HL 173, p.28.

The problem can be overcome by re-enacting the whole section, or subsection, of the relevant Act in the new bill in place of the usual approach of making amendments by reference only. [240] However, governments do not favour this because, in addition to debating the new wording of the bill, re-enactment risks opening up the debate about the wording of old statutes.

Introduction of a Keeling Schedule represents a useful solution to the problem by introducing a schedule to the bill that 'reproduces the provisions of the earlier measure and shows the effects of the amendments embodied in the bill'. [241] Although Keeling Schedules have the benefit of making amendments clear they do present some challenges. First, the Schedule must be kept accurate throughout the process of legislative scrutiny otherwise there will be a conflict between the words in two parts of the Act – those in the amending section and the new amended text set out in the Schedule. [242] There are also concerns that a Keeling Schedule represents duplication on the statute book and therefore, in the event of any subsequent amendments to the older Act, amendments may also be required to the enacted Keeling Schedule. [243] Finally, they impose a further heavy burden on Parliamentary Counsel in terms of drafting time and general resources.

The cost argument was rightly dismissed by the Lords Constitution Committee during its 2004 inquiry into the legislative process: 'cost cannot be taken as an insurmountable barrier to enhancing Parliament's capacity to engage in effective scrutiny of legislation. We believe that, in principle, members of both Houses should have the opportunity to see exactly how a bill amends an earlier Act.' [244]

The key question then is how effective scrutiny can best be facilitated. Successive governments have been reluctant to include Keeling Schedules into a bill itself, preferring instead an informal Keeling Schedule, produced either through an informal document published by the relevant government department setting out the details of the amended Act(s) or inclusion of details

---

[240] Lord Brightman (2002), 'Drafting Quagmires', *Statute Law Review*, 23(1), May 2002, p.4.

[241] House of Lords Constitution Committee (2003-04), *Parliament and the Legislative Process*, HL 173, p.27.

[242] *Ibid.*, Minutes of Evidence of 23 June, Q357.

[243] A. Samuels, 'Use of the Keeling Schedule', *Statute Law Review*, 18(3), November 1997, p.250.

[244] House of Lords Constitution Committee (2003-04), *Parliament and the Legislative Process*, HL 173, p.28.

of the amended Act in the explanatory notes accompanying a bill. [245] In both cases, the Keeling Schedule ceases to be of any use once the bill is enacted.[246] These two methods have the advantage of not having the force of law, for neither is part of the actual bill.

The use of informal Keeling Schedules has much support. Lord Norton recently recommended 'a Keeling-like Schedule' for the 2009-10 Digital Economy Bill's amendments to the Communications Act 2003. [247] When scrutinising the draft Local Transport Bill 2008, the Transport Committee recommended that Keeling Schedules be produced to accompany any bill that was introduced. [248] The government followed this recommendation publishing five schedules to the bill.

However, Keeling Schedules are not yet the 'norm'. As the example of the Academies Bill demonstrates, bills are still introduced where the level and complexity of amendments to previous legislation means a Keeling Schedule, whether formal or informal, would be of assistance while the proposed amendments are scrutinised. It seems that in cases where the Keeling Schedule is part of the explanatory notes the disadvantages of formally enacting such a Schedule are avoided but all the advantages retained.

We therefore recommend that Keeling-like Schedules become a standard element of explanatory notes to a bill, and be updated as the bill progresses through each stage of legislative scrutiny as required.

iii) Plain English

The general public, or even more specialised non-legal users, do not necessarily have a working knowledge of the principles and tools of statutory interpretation. They may have access to explanatory notes and other information materials but, further than this, the actual text of the law also needs to be as accessible as possible to the widest possible audience.

---

[245] For example, the Legislative Reform (Limited Partnerships) Order 2009 (SI 2009/1940) included a Keeling Schedule in the explanatory materials, showing the amended version of the Limited Partnerships Act 1907.

[246] House of Lords Constitution Committee (2003-04), *Parliament and the Legislative Process*, HL 173, Minutes of Evidence of 23 June, Q360.

[247] Lord Norton, 'Digital Economy Bill', *Lords of the Blog*, 2 December 2009, http://lordsoftheblog.net/2009/12/02/digital-economy-bill/

[248] House of Commons Transport Committee (2006-07), *The Draft Local Transport Bill and the Transport Innovation Fund*, paras 12-13.

To this end then it is often suggested that legislation should be produced in 'plain English' [249] which the Plain English Campaign defines as 'writing that the intended audience can read, understand and act upon the first time they read it'. [250] This can be done through use of explanations of technical terms, visual aids such as tables, use of the active rather than passive voice [251], use of short sentences [252] arranging provisions in time sequence [253] and keeping essential components together. They contend that legislation, in particular Acts of Parliament, on issues of wide public relevance such as employment law, should be drafted so that they can be read by as many people as possible. [254]

Statutes are not known for their concise use of language. Butt suggests that legal drafting has a tendency to 'ooze archaic language, illogical word order, complex grammatical structures, and sentences of excruciating length'. [255] Reliance on the previous version of an Act, when updating, [256] means that out-of-date language is copied into the new draft and despite intentions to adopt principles of plain language, a large percentage of the law on the statute books remains less than accessible. The effect of such verbosity in drafting means that the clarity of the bill is often compromised.

The effect of drafting law in impenetrable language is clear. As the Australian 'Plain English Manual' for Parliamentary Counsel sums up: 'If laws are hard to understand, they lead to administrative and legal costs, contempt of the law and criticism of our Office. Users of our laws are becoming increasingly impatient with their complexity. Further, if we put unnecessary difficulties in the

---

[249] 'Plain English' and 'plain language' are used interchangeably and taken to refer to the same broad concept.

[250] Plain English Campaign, 'Frequently asked questions', http://www.plainenglish.co.uk/faqs.html#Anchor-Wha-44708.

[251] 'The occupier leaves the premises' rather than 'the premises is left by the occupier'.

[252] Office of Parliamentary Counsel, Australia (2003), *Plain English Manual*, Chapter 3, http://www.opc.gov.au/about/docs/pem.pdf.

[253] 'Deal first with the application for a licence, then the issue of the licence, then the conditions of the licence...', *Ibid.*, para.105.

[254] Plain English Campaign, 'Drafting in plain English', http://www.plainenglish.co.uk/specialist-areas/legal/drafting-in-plain-english.html.

[255] P. Butt, 'Modern Legal Drafting', *Statute Law Review*, 23(1), May 2002, p.13.

[256] S. Laws, 'Drawing the Line', in C. Stefanou & H. Xanthaki (2008), *Drafting legislation: a modern approach* (London: Ashgate), p.27.

way of our readers, we do them a gross discourtesy. Finally, it's hard to take pride in our work if many people can't understand it.' [257]

But not everyone favours the use of plain language. While drafters may endorse the principle aim of making language clearer for the public to understand, the knock-on effects may not be so welcome. It is important to be clear that plain language does not in and of itself address the problem that legislation is complex. [258] Even apparently simple words may need to be explained in some detail in legislation, for example if a law applies to 'hot' food does this include a take-away meal that has gone cold before it is delivered? [259] This can therefore have the effect of increasing the overall length of the legislation, which itself can increase the number of different provisions that must be read to understand the position, and thereby lead to a loss of clarity. [260] Attempts to use plain language can also limit the legal effectiveness of the draft. Where only technical language is precise enough for some specialist users and the courts to understand, Parliamentary Counsel may see plain English as an unacceptable concession to legal effectiveness.

A further problem is that in changing the wording of an Act the interpretation of words in a previous statute on that subject might be lost. Greenberg notes however that the courts are now willing to reject suggestions that a change in wording necessarily means a change in meaning and some statutes explicitly provide that previous interpreting of case law will still apply. [261]

In other jurisdictions calls for plain language drafting have been met by providing Parliamentary Counsel with a manual to follow or external support. Since 1976 linguists in Sweden, for example, have examined all bills to ensure that they are drafted in accordance with plain language principles before they

---

[257] Office of Parliamentary Counsel, Australia (2003), *Plain English Manual*, para.5, http://www.opc.gov.au/about/docs/pem.pdf.

[258] J. Barnes, 'The continuing debate about 'plain language' legislation: a law reform conundrum', *Statute Law Review*, 27(2), 2006, p.118.

[259] Stephen Laws, First Parliamentary Counsel explained the need for defining the word 'hot' in detail in a Section of an Act then on the Plain English Campaign website. BBC Radio 4, *The Draftsman's Contract*, broadcast 17 December 2008, transcript at http://www.cabinetoffice.gov.uk/media/210695/draftsmanscontract2.pdf.

[260] R. Carter & M. Green, 'The enactment is self-explanatory – or is it? Explanatory provisions in New Zealand legislation', *Statute Law Review*, 28(1), April 2007, p.10.

[261] D. Greenberg (ed) (2008), *Craies on Legislation*, 9th edition (London: Sweet & Maxwell), para.8.1.

are sent for printing. The team also produces guidance and on-going training for drafters. But here in the UK an official plain English approach to drafting legislation has been slow to be adopted. The Office of Parliamentary Counsel has made some moves to simplifying language [262] and its Drafting Techniques Group has made recommendations such as avoiding long un-paragraphed sentences and words such as 'hereby'. [263] This guidance offers recommendations only and states that 'it is recognised that there will be times when drafters consider that, in the circumstances of the case, it would be appropriate to depart from a recommended approach'. [264] The OPC has also adopted gender-neutral drafting in recent years which they found, once they had started, 'was not nearly as difficult as we had thought it was'. [265]

In 2006 a trial was held to turn the provisions of the Coroners and Justice Bill into plain English. Although initially welcomed, this approach was dropped in later stages of the bill as the number of amendments that were introduced made the process increasingly difficult. However, this could be addressed by the addition of dates to the explanatory notes, so that even where they have not been fully updated to reflect amendments, it would be clear whether they refer to the latest version of the text, or not.

These small steps are welcome but have not made a great deal of difference to the overall product. In some cases there will always be a need for highly technical and precise language; yet in many other instances, an almost absurd level of terminology is used to describe straightforward concepts or terms. The challenge is to use plain language when it is possible, more legalistic terms sparingly as required, and to marry the two into a coherent workable whole. **We recommend that the government pilot some of the plain language drafting support models utilised overseas and continue to trial the use of plain English bills.**

---

[262] G. Bowman, 'Why is there a Parliamentary Counsel Office?', *Statute Law Review*, 26(2), 2005, p.79.

[263] Office of Parliamentary Counsel, *Recommendations and Policies on Drafting Matters*, pp.3-5, http://www.cabinetoffice.gov.uk/media/190037/dtg_recommendations250708.pdf.

[264] *Ibid.*, p.1

[265] BBC Radio 4, *The Draftsman's Contract*, broadcast 17 December 2008, transcript at http://www.cabinetoffice.gov.uk/media/210695/draftsmanscontract2.pdf.

iv) Explanatory materials

Explanatory notes have been prepared for every government bill [266] since the 1998-99 session in 'response to a demand for clearer law'. [267] Previously the only materials available were an explanatory memorandum which gave a broad description of the bill and some explanation of the constituent parts, but it was written in legal terms and had to be purchased with the bill. Recognising that 'no simple non-technical explanation is available to those potentially affected by the legislation' the House of Commons Modernisation Committee recommended their replacement with explanatory notes. [268] The Committee's paramount concern was that the notes should be written in plain English, avoid jargon, and be expressed in politically neutral terms. [269] Typically, explanatory notes will include an overview of the bill and its intentions, an outline of the events which have led to its introduction, clause-by-clause notes, an impact assessment, an assessment of the financial implications of the bill and information about the bill's compliance with the European Convention on Human Rights. The Cabinet Office 'Guide to Making Legislation' makes clear that their purpose is 'to make the bill accessible to readers who are not legally qualified and who have no specialised knowledge of the subject matter'. [270]

As explanatory notes do not form part of the bill itself they do not have full legal force (although the courts may look to them for guidance). It is therefore possible to draft them more freely, as there is less possibility of misconstruction. [271] In an effort to improve plain language communication of bills Parliament has also trialled the interleaving of the text of a bill with its explanatory notes so that the two texts appear in parallel on facing pages

---

[266] Explanatory notes are optionally included for finance bills, consolidation bills and Tax Law Rewrite bills. Cabinet Office, *Guide to making Legislation*, paras 11.1-11.3, http://www.cabinetoffice.gov.uk/making-legislation-guide/explanatory_notes.aspx.

[267] D. Greenberg (2009), *Access to legislation – the drafter's role*, www.cabinetoffice.gov.uk/media/274184/access.to.legislation.01.pdf.

[268] Select Committee on the Modernisation Committee of the House of Commons (1997-98), *The Legislative Process*, HC 190, para.34.

[269] *Ibid.*, para.37.

[270] Cabinet Office, *Guide to making Legislation*, para.11.9, http://www.cabinetoffice.gov.uk/making-legislation-guide/explanatory_notes.aspx.

[271] D. Greenberg (2009), *Access to legislation – the drafter's role*, www.cabinetoffice.gov.uk/media/274184/access.to.legislation.01.pdf.

rather than as separate documents. [272] However, it proved difficult to ensure that the notes remained accurate as amendments were made throughout the passage of the bill. [273] The use of explanatory notes has, however, been extended to notes on amendments during the passage of the bill. The aim was to provide members with briefing material setting out the intended effect of amendments prior to their debate in committee. As Greg Knight MP noted, they had a useful additional effect for they 'helped avoid the Public Bill Committee becoming a preserve of the front bench'. [274]

In general, explanatory notes are regarded as an asset to the scrutiny process. Some commentators fear, however, that MPs and peers are over-reliant on them and place too much emphasis on their contents, relying on the explanatory notes rather than the text of the bill itself for enlightenment. But this is perhaps understandable if the bill itself is impenetrable. Others, such as Greenberg, see the production of explanatory notes as a useful way for government to avoid dealing with the challenge of making bills themselves more accessible. [275] The need to make recourse to 'extrinsic materials' or other forms of interpretation is seen in some quarters as plain evidence of 'a failure by the drafter to ensure that the intention behind the new law is obvious.' [276] But as former First Parliamentary Counsel Christopher Jenkins explains, 'a bill is not there to inform, to explain, to entertain or to perform any of the other usual functions of literature. A bill's sole reason for existence is to change the law. The resulting Act is the law. A consequence of this unique function is that a bill cannot set about communicating with the reader in the same way that other forms of writing do.

---

[272] This was first trialled with the draft Coroners Bill in 2006 and the draft Marine Bill in 2008, and was used again with the Equality Bill in 2009. The Procedure Committee will assess the outcome of the experiment in due course and recommend whether bills should be published in this format in future. See House of Commons Procedure Committee (2008-09), *Interleaving of Bills and Explanatory notes*, HC 377.

[273] Cabinet Office, *Guide to making Legislation*, paras 11.14-11.24, http://www.cabinetoffice.gov.uk/making-legislation-guide/explanatory_notes.aspx.

[274] House of Commons Procedure Committee (2009-10), *Explanatory Statements on Amendments to Bills*, HC 420, p.2.

[275] See, for example, D. Greenberg (2009), *Access to legislation – the drafter's role*, www.cabinetoffice.gov.uk/media/274184/access.to.legislation.01.pdf.

[276] E. Moran, 'The relevance of statutory interpretation to drafting' in *Drafting for the 21st Century*, Conference at Bond University, Queensland, 6-8 February 1991, pp.100-109, cited in J. Barnes, 'The continuing debate about 'plain language' legislation: a law reform conundrum', *Statute Law Review*, 27(2), 2006, p.104.

It cannot use the same range of tools. In particular, it cannot repeat important points simply to emphasise their importance or safely explain itself by restating a proposition in different words. To do so would risk creating doubts and ambiguities that would fuel litigation. As a result, legislation speaks in a monotone and its language is compressed.' [277] Conversely, occasional concerns are sometimes raised that material that appears in the explanatory notes ought perhaps to appear in the legislation itself.

The quality of explanatory notes is not always a given. As one of our seminar participants put it, 'some look like they relate to another bill entirely'. Some commentators have expressed concerns about the quality of drafting, arguing that they often omit important information and have structural ambiguities. [278] The notes are drafted by the government department sponsoring the bill but must be reviewed and agreed by Parliamentary Counsel before publication. However, there is often a very short time available for this, with delays in the departments supplying them to the OPC and thence to Parliament. In other jurisdictions Parliamentary Counsel themselves draft the notes, for example, in Hong Kong. [279] An alternative model applies in New Zealand where the statement of purpose is drafted by Parliamentary Counsel, with the rest of the note drafted in the relevant government department. [280] Both options have their attractions, particularly ensuring that as far as possible all the drafting is done in one office; however there are cost and resource implications.

Parliament itself has no formal control over the notes [281] although members do, from time to time, seek amendments to them if they are dissatisfied with the quality of drafting. **On the whole, explanatory notes, while not perfect, have been a significant asset to the scrutiny process but more than 10**

---

[277] Select Committee on the Modernisation of the House of Commons (1997-98), *The Legislative Process*, HC 190, para.35.

[278] R. Munday, 'Explanatory notes and Statutory Interpretation', *Justice of the Peace*, 170 JPN 124, February 2006.

[279] Office of Parliamentary Counsel, Tasmania (2008), 'Guidelines for the Preparation of Statutory Rules', p.30, http://www.dpac.tas.gov.au/__data/assets/pdf_file/0005/48857/OPCMANUAL.pdf; Department of Justice, Hong Kong (2001), *Legislative Drafting in Hong Kong: Crystallization in Definitive Form*, 2nd edition, para.461, http://www.legislation.gov.hk/eng/pdf/ldhkv2.pdf.

[280] Office of Parliamentary Counsel, New Zealand (2010), *Guide to Working with Parliamentary Counsel*, edition 3.3, p.15, http://www.pco.parliament.govt.nz/assets/Uploads/pdf/guidetopco.pdf.

[281] Cabinet Office, 'Guide to making Legislation', para.11.10, http://www.cabinetoffice.gov.uk/making-legislation-guide/explanatory_notes.aspx.

years have passed since they were first introduced and there is some scope for revision and augmentation.

In order to improve the accessibility of bills and their comprehension by parliamentarians, given the large number of amendments tabled by government during the passage of bills, Parliament should require further explanatory statements be made to explain these changes on an on-going basis.

There are also lessons that could be learned from other parliamentary systems, such as in Scotland, where executive bills must usually be accompanied not only by an explanatory note, but also a policy memorandum, a financial memorandum and a memorandum on delegated powers.

The policy memorandum sets out the bill's policy objectives, what alternative approaches were considered, the consultations undertaken and an assessment of the effects of the bill on issues such as equal opportunities, human rights, island communities, local government, sustainable development and other matters considered relevant. While some of these points may be covered in the introduction to an explanatory note for a UK Parliament bill, the policy memoranda in Scotland are almost invariably longer and more detailed.

The financial memorandum sets out estimates of the expected costs of the bill to the Scottish administration (i.e. the executive, in the broad sense of ministers, departments and agencies), to local authorities and to other bodies, individuals and businesses. In each case, the memorandum indicates the timescales over which such costs are expected to arise and the margin of uncertainty in estimates given.

Executive bills in Scotland that contain provisions conferring powers to make subordinate legislation must also include a memorandum on delegated powers. This must set out:

- the person on whom any such power is conferred;

- the form in which the power is to be exercised;

- why it is considered appropriate to delegate the power;

- the parliamentary procedure (if any) to which the power is to be subject; and

- the reason for opting for that procedure.

The delegation of powers, especially to unelected officials or bodies, is often among the controversial elements of legislation, and therefore additional explanation up front by the executive about the precise details and reasons for such delegation could help facilitate an improved debate. Given the concern about the growing use of Henry VIII powers, such an approach could require government to clearly set out in such a memorandum why it has included them and how it envisions their use.

We believe that there should be a more comprehensive and clearly delineated model of explanatory materials to serve MPs and peers, which broadens the type and amount of information required in impact assessments and explanatory notes. We therefore recommend that Parliament introduce a revised model, at least on a trial basis, at the earliest opportunity. Such materials should be tied into the requirements of the Legislative Standards Committee which should assess whether the quality and detail of the explanatory materials is as required. Further information about how this might be done is set out in chapter 4.

v) Utilising technology

Greater use of technology could help parliamentarians better participate in detailed scrutiny in the Chamber and in committee, and particularly help them keep track of the effect of proposals when legislation is heavily amended by reference. Baroness Deech has suggested, for example, that some of the annunciators in the Chambers could be employed to show the proposed changes to the text of bills during the debate. [282] A more radical solution would be to make IT products – such as PDAs and tablet computers – available for use in the Chambers, each loaded with information about the business of the House that day and providing quick links between the various information sources that members might ideally consult in order to stay abreast of developments. Many other legislatures around the world – including, for example, the Scottish Parliament and the National Assembly for Wales – are designed in such a way as to provide computers and internet access to members at their desks in the Chamber. This is not the case at Westminster

---

[282] Baroness Deech during the Q&A discussion at the Hansard Society discussion forum for peers on 'Strengthening Parliament: reform of House of Lords procedure and governance', 14 July 2010, House of Lords.

but technology is now mobile and increasingly hand-held and therefore poses less of a challenge than in previous years. Given the many useful examples of the use of technology in other legislatures, the time may finally have come for Westminster to adopt innovations to enhance the work of MPs and peers. **Parliament should proactively explore, at least on a trial basis, how members might use such technology to better support the process of detailed legislative scrutiny.**

It is also axiomatic that for the laws of the land to be followed, they must be known by those who are affected by them. A long-standing complaint about the law in the United Kingdom is that there is not a free, up-to-date copy of the statute book available to the public. The new Legislation.gov.uk website (replacing the Office of Public Sector Information and Statute Law Database websites) contains the complete text of UK acts and statutory instruments from 1988 to the present day, but only partial copies of laws pre-dating 1988. The site also aims to provide up-to-date text of the law, reflecting amendments made to Acts and SIs by subsequent legislation, however this is still far from complete. It is therefore far from straightforward for a non-specialist to examine the text of law and be certain they are reading the most up-to-date version. While the Legislation.gov.uk site is new, its predecessors have been in a similar state of incompleteness for a number of years. It is imperative to the quality of the statute book and its accessibility to the public at large that investment is made in bringing its contents up-to-date.

Consolidation of law

Another mechanism that aids access to and understanding of the law is the consolidation of statutes or what Rogers and Walter have described as 'a sort of housekeeping of the statute book' to bring together existing law 'in a more logical and user-friendly way'. [283]

Here, several previous Acts or SIs on a particular subject are re-enacted as a single Act, not to change the law but to consolidate it into one place, facilitating a useful additional check on duplication and occasionally providing minor corrections and improvements. This has the obvious effect of making the law

---

[283] R. Rogers & R. Walters (2006), *How Parliament Works*, 6th Edition (Harlow: Pearson/Longman), p.210.

more accessible but also significantly clearer. Recommendations on the use of Consolidation Bills are made by the Law Commission who, with the support of Parliamentary Counsel loaned from the OPC, prepare bills for clearance by the government via the Cabinet Legislation Committee. Once approved, special procedures in Parliament then apply to facilitate a relatively smooth and efficient passage given that the bills are generally of a very technical nature rather than being concerned with policy. They are introduced to the House of Lords and remitted to the Joint Committee on Consolidation Bills after second reading. The Committee takes evidence from the drafter of the bill and the relevant government department, and then reports back to Parliament to confirm whether it deems the bill to be a pure consolidation measure representing the existing law or whether in fact there are any points of interest or concern that should be addressed. Where appropriate, the Committee can also make amendments to the bill to improve the consolidation. Following recommendation from the Joint Committee, the bills tend to pass quickly and with limited debate.

Consolidation may be desirable when the law on one subject has changed a great deal over time and therefore the body of law in that area is spread across many Acts, or where those Acts have lost their original structure due to multiple amendments. [284] It is a valuable tool to improve the quality of the statute book. As Lord Falconer emphasised in 2006, 'Consolidation is an important part of the government's better regulation agenda. It makes the law easier to use and understand. It improves the statute book and saves time and money for those who have to consult it.' [285]

However, despite the advantages of consolidation it has been used only sparingly and in narrow areas of legislation: between the 2001-02 and 2009-10 sessions, the committee reported on only eight bills for consolidation. [286] In large part this is because the process can be difficult and time-consuming. In

---

[284] The Law Commission (2009), *Annual Report 2008-09*, LC No. 316, HC 811, para.8.3.

[285] Lord Falconer, *Hansard*, 3 May 2006, vol. 681 col. 467.

[286] The Joint Consolidation Committee reported on: May 2008 – Statute Law (Repeals) Bill; July 2006 – the Parliamentary Costs Bill; the National Health Service Bill; the National Health Service (Wales) Bill'; the National Health Service (Consequential Provisions) Bill; May 2006 – the Wireless Telegraphy Bill; May 2004 – the Statute Law (Repeals) Bill; 2001 – the European Parliamentary Elections Bill. See www.parliament.uk/business/committees/committees-a-z/joint-select/consolidation-committee/publications/previous-sessions/

addition to the Acts to be consolidated, the effect of European law, devolution and the Human Rights Act 1998 must also be considered, all of which dampens ministerial appetite for the process. [287] The system is also not without its critics, for although minor amendments are possible, a Consolidation Act merely re-states existing law without changing it which means that, as Lord Phillips of Sudbury highlighted during consideration of the 2006 Wireless Telegraphy Act, 'We consolidate mistakes as well as everything else.' [288]

Overall however, the value of consolidation in improving the quality and accessibility of the statute book outweighs the disadvantages but pressures of time and political preferences for other legislative measures mean that consolidation initiatives are low on ministerial priority lists. **Consideration should therefore be given to requiring government departments to bring forward consolidation measures on a fixed basis or to report on the options for consolidation within their legislative remit on a regular timescale. One option would be to require a consolidation measure after a certain number of bills have been passed that amend the law in a particular area,** for example in the case of the Home Office's proliferation of immigration and asylum legislation over the last decade.

More broadly, the coalition government has committed itself to introduce a new Repeal Bill in the second session of Parliament from May 2012. This will be a substantial undertaking, not least to define acceptable criteria to determine what bills are obsolete or unnecessary. The work of the Law Commission should provide valuable assistance here as they have built up, over the last decade, a body of recommendations for codification, repeal and consolidation that have not yet been implemented by government and in some cases not yet even examined. **A new Repeal Bill on the scale proposed presents an historic opportunity to clean up the statute book. The government must ensure that the proposed legislation is fully consulted upon and properly scrutinised in Parliament to facilitate the widest possible engagement in the repeal exercise. It is imperative that improving the quality and integrity of the statute book is paramount and the exercise is not used simply as a populist tool to repeal a number of unpopular pieces of legislation.**

---

[287] The Law Commission (2009), *Annual Report 2008-09*, LC No. 316, HC 811, para.8.4.

[288] Lord Phillips of Sudbury in Joint Committee on Consolidation Bills (2005-06), *Wireless Telegraphy Bill [HL] – Volume II*, HL188-II, p.4.

Drafting and consolidating delegated legislation

The drafting of delegated legislation is generally carried out by departmental lawyers rather than Parliamentary Counsel. Unlike the OPC, departmental lawyers tend to draft in accordance with formal guidance for the production of SIs: this sets out the need to include headnotes, footnotes and information about the enabling powers in the Act. [289] In 2005 the government also issued a Statutory Instrument Practice Circular to departmental lawyers setting out modernisations to the drafting process that were to be implemented following liaison with the Joint Committee on Statutory Instruments. Henceforth, shorter and clearer preambles were required; archaisms such as 'hereafter' were to be omitted; Latin was to be avoided other than for important technical terms; and shorter sentences were required. As the circular noted, 'At times complexity is unavoidable because sufficient precision to give effect to the intended policy cannot be achieved otherwise. But that does not justify excessively long or complex sentences or use of surplus material, archaisms or unnecessarily formal terminology purely to follow precedent.' [290]

As with primary legislation, so too with delegated legislation there are serious concerns with regard to both volume and clarity and the impact this has on their accessibility to the user and broader audience. A 2006 Merits of Statutory Instruments Committee inquiry concluded that there was a tendency within government to amend previous SIs in such a way that it necessitated users referring to multiple documents at any one time in order to determine the exact legal position. [291] The committee recommended that, despite resource implications, there should be greater use of consolidating instruments. Its report also suggested improvements to explanatory memorandums, including that they be supervised by more senior staff. Two years later a follow-up report by the committee commended the increased provision of consolidated text in explanatory memorandums but

---

[289] Office of Public Sector Information (2006), *Statutory Instrument Practice*, paras 2.3, 2.11 & 3.43, http://www.opsi.gov.uk/si/si-practice.doc.

[290] D. Greenberg (ed) (2008), *Craies on Legislation*, 9th edition (London: Sweet & Maxwell), p.337.

[291] House of Lords Merits of Statutory Instruments Committee (2005-06), *The Management of Secondary Legislation*, HL 149, para.95.

recommended that more consolidation and simplification of delegated legislation needed to be undertaken. [292]

There have been suggestions from time to time that responsibility for drafting delegated legislation should be transferred to the OPC in order to ensure that all drafting of primary and secondary legislation takes place in one unit. However, as the Rippon Commission concluded in 1993, the existing arrangements have some benefits. [293] For example, the majority of SIs deal with issues of practical administration linked to the application of legislation and these are matters that departmental lawyers are more familiar with than are Parliamentary Counsel. The legal content of SIs is also generally less than in bills. The suggestion that Parliamentary Counsel draft delegated legislation would significantly increase their workload, and have a considerable knock-on effect on requirements for team expansion and resourcing. On balance, the existing arrangements are perhaps preferable given that the biggest problem with delegated legislation is not the quality of the drafted Instruments but the significance of their policy and administrative content that is ultimately a matter for ministers. The specific concerns about the clarity and accessibility of SIs apply equally as much to primary legislation drafted by the OPC so there are no reasons to assume that shifting drafting responsibility would ease the problem. **Clarity can be improved by greater use of consolidation of instruments and we recommend that this be considered by ministers as part of their broader purview of work in relation to the proposed Repeal Bill.**

The Tax Law Rewrite Project

Given that mechanisms for consolidation and improving access to statutes are sparsely used, there is scope for exploring what innovative models might be utilised more widely to accomplish the aims of improving the understanding of statutes in certain areas of law and thereby enhancing access to it. The Tax Law Rewrite Project is one such model. It has gone beyond a traditional consolidation of legislation to provide for whole-scale revision of a highly complex, technical area of the law. While the project has been time-consuming

---

[292] House of Lords Merits of Statutory Instruments Committee (2007-08), *The Management of Secondary Legislation: Follow-up*, HL 70, paras 26-29.

[293] Hansard Society (1993), *Making the Law: The Report of the Hansard Society Commission on the Legislative Process* (London: Hansard Society), paras 187-189.

and resource-heavy, the end result has been an improvement in access to and clarity of tax law, and other discrete areas of existing law might benefit from similar attention.

As a result of repeated amendment, tax law has over many years become much longer and more structurally complex as it has responded to the need to address newly emerging social issues and concepts (the changing nature of family life and structure, for example), an increase in regulatory frameworks, changes to the general legal framework and an increasing desire for precision in the law in order to limit the scope for officer discretion in its application at the front-line of service delivery. In 1970, for example, it was estimated that tax measures were enshrined in 2,000 pages of law; by 1996 this had grown to 6,000 pages and has continued to expand in the years since. [294] Even expert practitioners who use it regularly note that the meaning of some tax law is not always apparent: as one accountant commented 'When you use ICTA [Income and Corporation Taxes Act 1988] you think "bloody hell, I really don't understand what this means".' [295]

The initial proposal to rewrite primary direct taxation legislation can be discerned in the parliamentary discussions of the 1995 Finance Bill. A backbench amendment proposing a clause to require the Inland Revenue to publish a report on the length and complexity of the Revenue tax code was agreed in the 1995 Finance Act. The resulting report – 'The Path to Tax Simplification' – was published later that year and core to its recommendations was that primary legislation should be rewritten using simpler, more accessible, user-friendly language. A consultation took place over the course of the following year and in the 1996 Budget the Chancellor Kenneth Clarke MP announced the establishment of the Tax Law Rewrite Project with a remit to 'rewrite the UK's primary direct tax legislation to make it clearer and easier to use, without changing the law'. [296] The initial plan was to do so in the form of a consolidation measure but the project rapidly extended beyond this to encompass the need to 'modernise and simplify the whole language, style, format and presentation' [297]

---

[294] See G. Howe, 'Tax Law Simplification in the United Kingdom' in C. Sandford (ed) (1998), *Further Key Issues in Tax Reform* (Bath: Fiscal, Bath), p.89.

[295] MORI (2006), *The Income Tax (Earnings and Pensions) Act 2003 – Post-implementation Review Research Study for HM Customs and Revenue*, p.10, www.hmrc.gov.uk/rewrite/itepa-final-report.pdf.

[296] HM Revenue & Customs, 'Tax Law Rewrite', http://www.hmrc.gov.uk/rewrite/

[297] A. Samuels, 'Consolidation: A Plea', *Statute Law Review*, 26(1), 2005, p.59.

and to develop new drafting techniques which could be used in other legislative drafting. [298] It was originally envisaged that the project would take five years to complete but the growing remit meant this was insufficient and in fact it only came to an end in 2010. With approximately 30 members of staff at any one time, the project team drew on expertise through officers from HM Revenue and Customs, tax professionals who had been working in private practice and Parliamentary Counsel. There was also a steering committee chaired by former Chancellor of the Exchequer, Lord Howe of Aberavon, and a consultative committee to engage the support and advice of a range of professional expertise on the amendments proposed. [299]

Initially the project consulted on the management and principles of the rewrite, and drafting techniques, including whether purposive drafting should be utilised and in what order the subjects should be rewritten. The drafting techniques agreed by the team included:

- adding signposts and worked examples to the rewrite in order to aid understanding – this was for explanatory purposes and did not have legal force; [300]

- using formulae to illustrate calculations, rather than words, with these taking full legal effect; [301]

- use of modern language and gender-neutral drafting wherever possible provided it could be done without changing the law or rendering its effect less certain; [302]

- using purposive drafting; [303]

---

[298] HM Revenue & Customs, 'Tax Law Rewrite; Report and Plans 2007/08', http://webarchive. nationalarchives.gov.uk/20100407044210/http://www.hmrc.gov.uk/rewrite/plans2007-08.htm.

[299] H. Rogers, 'Drafting Legislation at the Tax Law Rewrite Project', in C. Stefanou & H. Xanthaki (2008), *Drafting legislation: a modern approach* (London: Ashgate), p.77.

[300] *Ibid.*, p.82

[301] *Ibid.*, p.81

[302] HM Revenue & Customs, 'Tax Law Rewrite – Plans for 1997', para.3.5, http://webarchive. nationalarchives.gov.uk/20100407044210/http://www.hmrc.gov.uk/rewrite/plans97/chap3.htm.

[303] The 'Plans for 1997' document states that this term is used to include 'general statements of principle, with few detailed rules in the primary legislation'. Use of purposive drafting was decided to be limited to situations where this would not cause uncertainty. HM Revenue & Customs, 'Tax Law Rewrite – Plans for 1997', para.3.20, http://webarchive.nationalarchives.gov.uk/20100407044210/ http://www.hmrc.gov.uk/rewrite/plans97/chap3.htm.

The project consulted widely, particularly with policy experts and practitioners, producing draft clauses in sections for each rewrite bill they proposed, and published detailed responses to each consultation including a summary of the comments they had received and how the project responded to these. [304] Although the Rewrite Bills were in large part consolidating measures, they did not qualify for the Consolidation Bill process in Parliament because the scale of the project meant accidental changes to the law could be introduced. The bills were also deemed unsuitable for the normal Finance Bill procedure for fear that the sheer volume of legislation the project produced would result in a re-opening of the general debate about tax policy. A special, streamlined procedure was therefore created on the recommendation of the Procedure Committee. [305] On introduction to Parliament the bills were referred to a second reading committee and then to a new Joint Committee on Tax Law Rewrite Bills. Following report by the Joint Committee, and a third reading, bills were then scrutinised by the House of Lords and received Royal Assent in a matter of weeks. [306]

Overall, the response to the project was generally positive. Consolidation was deemed a success for having made tax law much easier to navigate by users, leading many practitioners to conclude that there would be time and other resource savings to be made by them as a result. Some had reservations, focused largely on the fact that the Rewrite Project concentrated on linguistic and structural changes and therefore did not address key areas they believed were the real problem in terms of the overall complexity of tax policy itself. [307] Some were also sceptical about the benefit of a dedicated project instead of utilising a normal consolidation procedure. As Tiley argued, 'One comes away from the draft bill thinking, uncharitably, that there is much here that could have been covered by an intelligent consolidation.' [308] And although the project may

[304] Opinion Leader Research (2003), *Inland Revenue Evaluation of the Capital Allowances Act 2001 rewrite*, (London: Opinion Leader Research), para.4.3.1, http://www.hmrc.gov.uk/rewrite/caa-01-rolre.pdf.

[305] House of Commons Procedure Committee (1996-97), *Legislative Procedure for Tax Simplification Bills*, HC 126.

[306] House of Commons Library (2001), *Tax Law Rewrite: Capital Allowances Bill*, Research Paper 01/04, 11 January 2001, pp.33-41.

[307] See, for example, MORI (2006), *The Income Tax (Earnings and Pensions) Act 2003 – Post-implementation Review Research Study for HM Customs and Revenue*, p.12, www.hmrc.gov.uk/rewrite/itepa-final-report.pdf, accessed 23 November 2010 and M. Truman (2007), 'Hardman Lecture', Institute of Chartered Accountants in England and Wales, London, para.5.2.

[308] J. Tiley, 'Exercising their Write', 741 Tax Journal 11, May 2004.

have simplified navigation of tax law it actually resulted in a further lengthening of the statute book. However, clarity rather than a reduction in volume was always the primary purpose of the project and on balance it is widely regarded as having achieved its objectives. As Rogers argued, 'the view has been that the increased length will be more than outweighed by the gains in clarity'. [309]

The Tax Law Rewrite Project offers a model that could be utilised for a systematic approach to the rewriting of other complex, highly technical areas of law in order to achieve greater clarity of the statute book in a broader range of policy areas. **Although time-consuming and expensive, ministers, alongside preparatory work for the Repeal Bill, should consider this Rewrite Project approach for other areas of legislation.**

---

[309] H. Rogers, 'Drafting Legislation at the Tax Law Rewrite Project', in C. Stefanou & H. Xanthaki (2008), *Drafting legislation: a modern approach* (London: Ashgate), p.80.

Chapter 4: Reform and innovation in legislative scrutiny

The quality of law is ultimately shaped by the scrutiny it receives in Parliament. And despite a belief within government that to change a bill is a sign of weakness, 'Parliament, as a whole and through its constituent parts, does make a difference to legislation, sometimes in major ways, and more frequently through many minor but significant changes.' [310]

But while some aspects of Parliament's scrutiny process work effectively to improve legislation, there are a number of structural, procedural and cultural issues in Parliament that could be reformed to make its work better and improve the quality of laws it passes.

While the consideration of bills is largely dominated by partisan battle, the key relationship in the legislative process is between Parliament and the executive. To enhance the scrutiny of bills, and thus improve the quality of legislation, Parliament needs to take greater control of the legislative process, stand up to government more often, and make better use of the existing tools and procedures available to it.

The preceding chapters have highlighted the issues in the policy-making, consultation, and drafting process that impact upon the quality of legislation that reaches Parliament. While the recommendations outlined would go a long way to improving matters, it is unlikely that they would solve the problem of poor quality legislation in its entirety. Parliament must always be alert to the prospect of bills arriving at its door in need of work.

Chapter 1 highlighted in particular the tidal wave of legislation that Parliament is asked to scrutinise and established that its capacity to do so on the scale required is severely stretched.

It would ameliorate this situation considerably if Parliament were able to identify poorly prepared legislation and return it to government for revision before commencing the legislative process proper. This however, is far from

---

[310] A. Brazier, S. Kalitowski & G. Rosenblatt with M. Korris (2008), *Law in the Making: Influence and Change in the Legislative Process* (London: Hansard Society), pp.4-5.

straightforward to achieve, as it requires not just incisive scrutiny to identify flawed bills but involves challenging the executive's right to introduce legislation to Parliament. It also requires members of the governing party (or parties) to be willing to challenge their own government on these matters, something that the tribal nature of the Commons makes it very difficult to do.

Raising legislative standards

In government the Cabinet's Parliamentary Business and Legislation Committee (or PB Committee) is the gatekeeper for prospective legislation before it goes to Parliament. However, too often its safeguards are by-passed for reasons of short-term political advantage by ministers. Parliament, in contrast, does not have any gate-keeping mechanism of its own to decline to consider poorly prepared legislation. The terms of political engagement between Whitehall and Westminster at present require that Parliament consider whatever legislation the government sends them, whenever they send it, and regardless of the condition in which it is sent. This is a certain recipe for the continued receipt of poorly prepared bills and therefore the production of defective laws. Parliament should be a more equal partner in the legislative process working with government to mutually agreed qualifying standards of bill preparation. The right of the executive to implement its legislative programme should be qualified only by the right of Parliament to decline to scrutinise legislation that is not in a fit state for consideration. But that scope for objection should be clearly defined and limited such that it cannot be used by the opposition for their own partisan purposes to derail the government's programme.

Parliament should therefore establish its own gateway Legislative Standards Committee, ideally on a bi-cameral basis, to assess bills against a set of minimum technical preparation standards that all bills should be required to meet before introduction is permitted. The committee should agree those standards – narrow, tightly drawn, objective qualifying criteria that establish a minimum threshold for bill preparation – in consultation with the government. Before legislation is presented to the committee the relevant departmental Secretary of State or the Leader of the House should be required to certify that they believe the bill does indeed meet those qualifying standards. The committee should then judge the bill according to the agreed criteria, assessing the legislation purely on the basis of whether the legislative standards of bill preparation have been met, not whether they believe the policy objectives are likely to be realised or whether the principles and policies enshrined in the legislation are appropriate. The Legislative Standards Committee would have the option to call ministers to appear before it to account for their department's preparation of the bill. It would then submit a report setting out its recommendations before second reading and it would be for the relevant House to decide whether or not to defer a bill if the preparation criteria are deemed by the committee not to have been met. In some instances the House may decide to proceed with the bill despite the committee's concerns: but in these instances the decision will lie with the House and it will have taken the decision in an informed manner.

As part of this pre-introduction process, **Parliament should also require more detailed information from government regarding the bill, as is required, for example, in the Scottish Parliament.** At present, impact assessments on equality, competition, and a range of environmental, health and human rights are all required. In addition, we suggest that **a new Legislative Impact Assessment should also be demanded by Parliament.** This would include a history of past legislation in the area; make clear that the powers requested do not already exist in statute; identify where shortcomings exist and need to be rectified and confirm that these can only be dealt with by new, additional legislation as opposed to other governmental action; and evaluate whether and when consolidation may be required. It should also call the government to account for any delegated legislation proposals – including Henry VIII powers – set out in the bill. The Legislative Standards Committee should look to the example of the Scottish Parliament to see how the other supporting materials that accompany bills might be improved. For example, what information requirements contained in Scottish delegated powers memoranda might be transferred into a Westminster Legislative Impact Assessment and what additional information and subject areas might be drawn from Scottish policy memoranda for inclusion in Westminster explanatory notes (see chapter 3). As well as informing the work of parliamentarians when scrutinising the bill as it goes through its various legislative stages, improved supporting materials might also be a useful aide-memoire for members to reference when, some years later, they undertake post-legislative scrutiny of the resulting Act.

The combined existence of the committee coupled with agreed minimum standards for legislative preparation which ministers would have to certify had been met when submitting a bill should provide, over time, an important restraining influence on government with regard to the quality of bills being produced and thereby help to better rebalance the relationship between the executive and Parliament.

An alternative, though weaker, option to achieve the same outcome would be to require government to table a motion to bring in a government bill. This would therefore require Parliament to pass a motion approving the introduction of a bill for a specified purpose. At the point of introduction this would allow the relevant House to question ministers about, for instance, the need to repeatedly legislate on the same area of policy (as in the example of the Home Office in chapter 1) and delay or even reject a bill. This mechanism exists in some form in relation to the Finance Bill. At the end of the final day of debate on the Budget, the House of Commons passes a series of short, in-principle resolutions (often just one line long) to approve the measures contained in the Budget policy document. At the end it is 'Ordered, That a Bill be brought in upon the foregoing Resolutions', and the first reading of the resultant Finance Bill is taken.

However, this process has a number of shortcomings. Firstly, the time between the motion being passed and the arrival of the bill (straight afterwards, with second reading usually scheduled for the following day) is short. While it allows Parliament, in theory, to reject the resolutions that make up the Finance Bill, it does not allow the opportunity for any constructive criticism before the legislative process begins. Alternatively, if a motion to introduce a bill was required several months in advance of its introduction then not only would the government's position be more flexible (as it is in the case of pre-legislative scrutiny as set out below) but it would provide time for parliamentarians, particularly select committees, and outsiders to better prepare for scrutiny of the intended subject area. There will always, however, be instances when governments want and need to legislate more quickly than this and cannot provide advance notice of their intention to bring forward a bill. But perhaps the biggest flaw in this 'motion to bring in a government bill' process is that it does not provide for the use of any objective qualifying criteria about standards of legislative preparation. Whether or not the motion to bring in a bill passes will be solely based on the ability of the government to marshal its votes in the relevant House. Debate about the bill will also likely resemble the second reading debate on the principles of the bill and whether members agree with them. Rather than this duplicative form of scrutiny, what is actually needed at the introduction stage is a technical assessment of the readiness of the legislation. So although there are some attractions in the use of a motion prior to introduction, a gateway Legislative Standards Committee provides both a more appropriate and a stronger solution to the actual problem that Parliament faces, namely the current introduction of defective bills.

Managing time

Allowing sufficient time for scrutiny of a bill is a key element in the process of making better law. More time is not sufficient in itself to result in the improvement of a bill; other reforms outlined here are also required if this is to be achieved. But if the provision of time is not maximised and used more effectively and rationally during each stage of deliberation, then the potential impact that any procedural reforms might have on the process of making better law will be reduced concomitantly.

Time is at a premium across the parliamentary session as a whole and in relation to individual bills. There is only limited scope for expanding the parliamentary calendar and sitting times, but the use and management of time within the current parameters could certainly be improved. As one senior parliamentary official has put it 'there is no more time in the system; the question is how to use it more effectively'. [311] Of course, introducing fewer and shorter bills into Parliament is the most effective way of allowing more time for scrutiny.

i) A legislative not a sessional cycle

At present, the legislative timetable is dealt with on a sessional basis. As outlined in chapter 1, this provides a cut-off point beyond which legislation, if it has not completed all the scrutiny stages, must either be carried-over or be lost. A number of large, highly significant bills have been carried over in recent years, for example: the Welfare Reform Bill in 2006; the Criminal Justice and Immigration Bill in 2007; the Banking Bill in 2008 and the Equality Bill and the Constitutional Reform and Governance Bill, both in 2009. But the number of bills carried over as a proportion of the entire legislative programme remains small. **There is scope for much greater use of the sessional carry-over procedure.**

It was suggested at our fourth and final seminar on innovations in legislative scrutiny that one solution to the management of time problem

---

[311] *Ibid.*, p.194.

would be to take an entirely new approach to the concept of a session and the legislative cycle. Assuming the ideal scrutiny model – in which each bill would receive pre-legislative scrutiny – bills, once introduced in draft, should be considered on a two-year cycle in which the first year dealt with the pre-legislative consultation phase with the legislative scrutiny stages then dealt with in the second year. This would pose challenges to the management of business but as one seminar participant stressed, 'it would mean legislation would not be on a mechanistic convoy in which everything runs at the same speed'.

There was some concern that this would extend the legislative cycle too much as the earlier policy and drafting preparation by government would need to be added to the two-year period, in effect extending it to a three-year cycle. However, the principle of time constraints being determined differently for each bill in accordance with their date of introduction – in effect providing an independent rolling session for each bill up to an agreed maximum number of months – would address the current problem whereby detailed consideration of many bills comes to an abrupt end at the close of the session when measures are rushed through their remaining stages to avoid the legislation being lost. It would also retain the cut-off feature – which government and opposition can find advantageous for different reasons as outlined in chapter 1 – but the actual cut-off date would be determined by the timing of the bill's introduction, not the rigidities of the parliamentary sessional calendar. And, as now, there should be provision for the introduction of legislation on a fast-track timetable – albeit within clearly agreed parameters as set out later in this chapter – if required.

The government's proposals to introduce a Fixed Term Parliament and its decision to extend the first session of this Parliament to May 2012 in order to rationalise sessional times in accordance with the proposed end date of this Parliament in 2015 provide an opportunity to manage legislative business better and to think more radically about how this might be done. If the management of bills were moved to a legislative rather than a sessional cycle then some consideration would need to be given to what this means for the House of Lords in relation to their use of the Parliament Act, the use of which is defined in sessional terms. However, this should not be an insurmountable problem. **We therefore recommend that the Procedure Committee should explore the merits of moving consideration of bills to a legislative rather than a sessional cycle.**

ii) Programming

Timetabling is used in the House of Commons to ensure that the business of legislation is managed efficiently and effectively. It needs to strike a careful balance between the right of government to enact its legislative programme efficiently and the importance of effective scrutiny of bills by members.

Prior to 1997, the timing of the various stages of the legislative process was managed primarily by allocation of time motions – a process colloquially known as the 'guillotine'. Debates on a bill would continue until the government sought to conclude it with a guillotine, irrespective of how much of the bill had been debated. This situation was patently unsatisfactory. In 1985 the Procedure Committee argued for the introduction of a new system of formal timetabling of business [312] and in 1993 the Hansard Society's Rippon Commission concurred, and recommended that a Business Committee also be established in conjunction with it. [313] The aim was to introduce more certainty into the legislative process and to eradicate, or at least greatly reduce, the gaps in scrutiny that occurred when a bill ran out of time, resulting in many clauses being left undebated under the old procedure.

A trial system of 'programming' legislation was established in 1997 on the recommendation of the Modernisation Committee, but in practice programming motions were not frequently used until after 2000. [314] The committee argued that the new system would be 'more formal' than the usual channels but 'more flexible than the guillotine'[315] and in reviews in 2000, and again in 2003, it set out the principles by which the system should operate:

'a) The Government of the day must be assured of getting its legislation through in a reasonable time (provided that it can obtain the approval of the House);

b) The Opposition in particular, and Members in general, must have a full opportunity to discuss and seek to change provisions to which they attach importance;

[312] House of Commons Procedure Committee (1984-85), *Public Bill Procedure*, HC 49.

[313] Hansard Society (1993), *Making the Law: The Report of the Hansard Society Commission on the Legislative Process* (London: Hansard Society), p.123 & p.150.

[314] A. Brazier (2004), *Issues in Law Making 4: Programming of Legislation* (London: Hansard Society).

[315] Select Committee on the Modernisation of the House of Commons (1997-98), *The Legislative Process*, HC 190.

c)   All parts of a bill must be properly considered;

d)   Bills need to be prepared properly so as not to require a mass of new Government amendments.' [316]

The programming of bills has been an improvement over the allocation of time motions (guillotines) which were largely used previously, in that it has afforded greater certainty to the timetable for legislative scrutiny, and guaranteed that the first principle – the right of the government to get its legislation through in reasonable time – has been achieved. Indeed, one of the key criticisms of the way programming operates is that it has strengthened the executive precisely because it deprives the opposition of one of its rare parliamentary weapons, namely time, and therefore the ability to obstruct and delay legislation.

But it is clear that the rest of the Modernisation Committee's principles have not been met. [317] Programming is now used for almost every government bill, but since 2001 it has rarely been consensual. [318] Opposition and backbench members often consider that insufficient time is available for scrutiny leading to the contesting of programme motions. As a consequence, significant amounts of parliamentary time are now eaten up debating the programme motion itself; time that could be better spent on scrutiny of the legislation at issue. Large numbers of bill clauses still go undebated in the Commons and large numbers of amendments are still required. Programming bites particularly harshly at report stage where a majority of bills receive only one day of debate rather than the preferred two, which, taken together with the government's increasing tendency to table a significant number of late amendments, makes detailed scrutiny particularly difficult.

The problems with programming exemplify what can happen when a reform is introduced in isolation, decoupled from other reforms intended to accompany it as part of a broad package of change. When the Rippon Commission recommended the introduction of timetabling, it saw this reform in the context

---

[316] Select Committee on the Modernisation of the House of Commons (1999–2000), *Programming of Legislation and Timing of Votes*, HC 589, para.5; Select Committee on the Modernisation of the House of Commons (2002–03), *Programming of Bills*, HC 1222, para.11.

[317] A. Brazier, S. Kalitowski & G. Rosenblatt with M. Korris (2008), *Law in the Making: Influence and Change in the Legislative Process* (London: Hansard Society).

[318] House of Commons Procedure Committee (2003-04), *Programming of Legislation*, HC 325; House of Commons Procedure Committee (2008-09), *Timetabling of Business – Memorandum submitted by the Hansard Society*, TB 07.

of other proposed changes, particularly greater use of pre-legislative scrutiny, carry-over of legislation, and the introduction of a Business Committee. The use of pre-legislative scrutiny and carry-over has not been as envisaged by the Commission and the proposal for a Business Committee, after many years in the wilderness, has only recently re-emerged on the political agenda following its recommendation by the Select Committee on Reform of the House of Commons (the Wright Committee). [319]

The issue of programming has been the subject of repeated analysis by the Hansard Society in the years since its introduction. [320] As in previous reports, we again **recommend that a major review of the operation of programming be undertaken with a view to rebalancing the timetabling of business in favour of Parliament and improved time for scrutiny**. [321]

Linked to this, we urge the government to restore a collaborative cross-party approach to the timetabling of business. To encourage a more co-operative approach between the parties, hurdles might be introduced for those times when agreement on programming is not reached, such as, for example, a full day's debate on the programme motion. [322] This would build into the system a considerable disincentive such that it would be rarely in any party's interest to deliberately undermine the collaborative approach.

iii) Business Committee

For many years the Hansard Society and other bodies have urged that one of the most effective long-term solutions to improve the management of time in the House of Commons would be through the introduction of a Business

---

[319] See Reform of the House of Commons Committee (2008-09), *Rebuilding the House*, HC 1117.

[320] See Hansard Society (2001), *The Challenge for Parliament; Making Government Accountable, Report of the Hansard Society Commission on Parliamentary Scrutiny* (London: Vacher Dod), pp.25-26; A. Brazier (2004), *Issues in Law Making 4: Programming of Legislation* (London: Hansard Society); A. Brazier (ed) (2004), *Parliament, Politics and Law Making: Issues & Developments in the Legislative Process* (London: Hansard Society); A. Brazier, M. Flinders & D. McHugh (2005), *New Politics, New Parliament?* (London: Hansard Society).

[321] A. Brazier, S. Kalitowski & G. Rosenblatt with M. Korris (2008), *Law in the Making: Influence and Change in the Legislative Process* (London: Hansard Society), p.205.

[322] R. Rogers & O. Gay, 'Suggestions for possible changes to the procedure and business of the House – a note by the Clerks', House of Commons Parliament and Constitution Research Centre note, SN/PC/05110, 18 June 2009, para.c.7, p.6.

Committee. [323] Instead of the government having complete control of the management of legislation in the Commons and the opaque operation of the 'usual channels' [324] (the party business managers) a Business Committee would represent the voices of the opposition and backbenchers in the process, operate transparently, and thus challenge the government to justify the timing of individual bills and legislation throughout the parliamentary session.

A Business Committee has the potential to significantly improve the arrangement of legislative business in the House of Commons, leading to enhanced scrutiny and thereby contributing to the process of making better law. Many other legislatures organise their legislative process in a way that allows the government's need for legislative time to be balanced with both opposition and backbench concerns.

A Business Committee was a key recommendation of the Wright Committee [325] and the coalition government has undertaken to establish such a committee within three years. [326] However, it is not clear at this stage what form the committee will take, how it will be composed and what remit and powers it will have.

In order to tackle the issues of time within the legislative process, **we recommend that a Business Committee should be established as promised within three years and be designed to meet the following principles:**

- provide greater certainty to the parliamentary timetable;

- ensure that the government will be able to secure its legislative programme;

- offer greater involvement by the parties in the management of business;

- facilitate greater discussion and involvement of all interested parties in the Commons in the shaping and timing of the legislative programme; and

- establish greater transparency in the overall process.

---

[323] For example, see M. Russell & A. Paun (eds) (2006), *Managing Parliament Better? A Business Committee for the House of Commons* (London: Constitution Unit); M. Russell & A. Paun (2007), *The House Rules? International lessons for enhancing the autonomy of the House of Commons* (London: Constitution Unit).

[324] See M. Rush & C. Ettinghausen (2002), *Opening Up the Usual Channels* (London: Hansard Society).

[325] Reform of the House of Commons Committee (2008-09), *Rebuilding the House*, HC 1117. A Backbench Business Committee to choose the topics for debates in non-government time, which was also a recommendation of this Committee, was established at the beginning of the new parliamentary session in 2010.

[326] HM Government (2010), *The Coalition: our programme for government*, p.27.

The committee should be composed of representatives of all parties, with representation weighted to reflect the strength of the parties in Parliament. It might be chaired by the Speaker or the Deputy Speaker (Chair of Ways and Means). A clear demarcation between the executive's share of the parliamentary timetable and the share allocated for all other parliamentary activity should be determined, as is the case with the time now allocated for determination by the newly-formed Backbench Business Committee. The executive will thus remain assured of securing its business but the system of managing that business will be placed on a formal, transparent footing.

A key objective of the Business Committee should be to link the application of programming motions more explicitly to other elements of the legislative process in order to incentivise the adoption of an improved approach by the executive in the interests of making better law. For example, with the exception of certain bills by prior agreement (such as the Finance Bill), it could require mandatory pre-legislative scrutiny for all bills unless it was overridden by a motion requiring a qualified majority vote in the House. [327] Alternatively, if a bill has not been considered in draft it might be committed to a new mandatory select committee stage prior to second reading. [328] Or perhaps programme motions might only be moved immediately after second reading without debate if at least one of the following four conditions had been met: (a) the bill had been subject to pre-legislative scrutiny; (b) the bill is to be subject to carry-over between sessions (to increase the overall time for scrutiny); (c) the bill is to be committed to a Committee of the Whole House; (d) there is cross-party agreement on the terms of the programme. [329]

iv) Time-saving strategies

Looking at the parliamentary timetable more broadly, there are a range of time-saving strategies that Parliament could utilise now to improve the efficiency of its operation, thus freeing up time each week for more detailed scrutiny, and

---

[327] There is precedence for such a reform as closure motions used to require a three to one vote.

[328] R. Rogers & O. Gay, 'Suggestions for possible changes to the procedure and business of the House – a note by the Clerks', House of Commons Parliament and Constitution Research Centre note, SN/PC/05110, 18 June 2009, para.d.5, p.9.

[329] A. Brazier (ed) (2004), *Parliament, Politics and Law Making: Issues & Developments in the Legislative Process* (London: Hansard Society), pp.26-27.

particularly to facilitate more time in the Chamber itself where the focus should fall on the more contentious aspects of legislation rather than general, often anodyne debates.

The setting of time limits for speeches should be left in the hands of the Speaker. The Speaker is in the best position to make a judgement on an appropriate time limit, on the basis of the representations he or she receives from backbenchers who wish to participate in debate. If the model of a Business Committee with the Speaker as chair is adopted, then time limits could be proposed by the Speaker and agreed with members.

Another time-saving measure for the main Chamber of the House of Commons would be to **move the second reading stage of uncontroversial bills to Westminster Hall, contingent on the agreement of all the main parties (and the Business Committee when it is established).** Votes on second readings could be taken under the current procedure of deferred divisions. **This too would be an option for some of the poorly-attended general debates that take place in the Commons Chamber, especially those on adjournment motions.** While the topicality and interest of issue-driven debates will hopefully improve as a result of the establishment of the Backbench Business Committee, many currently attract few MPs and could be moved to Westminster Hall to free up time for legislative scrutiny.

v) Fast-track legislation

While there is usually insufficient time for scrutiny during the legislative process, the problems are severely exacerbated when the government introduces fast-track legislation. Here the government seeks to contract the legislative process by conducting the various stages as quickly as possible in order to get a bill through Parliament on an expedited timetable. Often described as emergency legislation, this may be introduced for a variety of reasons, such as to remedy an anomaly or error in existing legislation, to respond to a court judgement, to react to unforeseen events, or to respond to an emerging public concern. [330]

While the justification for fast-track legislation may in some instances be widely supported, the foreshortening of the scrutiny processes in Parliament creates a

---

[330] House of Lords Constitution Committee (2008-09), *Fast-track Legislation: Constitutional Implications and Safeguards*, HL 116.

real risk of enacting poor quality legislation. The Dangerous Dogs Act 1991 is a classic example of a bill being rushed through Parliament to satisfy public and media pressure but which badly failed to achieve its desired ends in practice.

A number of safeguards are urgently required to ensure that legislation subject to a fast-track through Parliament is subject to adequate scrutiny and reviewed subsequent to Royal Assent. **Having decided to introduce fast-track legislation the government should have to fully justify its reasons for doing so.** The House of Lords Constitution Committee recommended that a ministerial statement should be required to address the following principles:

'(a)   Why is fast-tracking necessary?

(b)   What is the justification for fast-tracking each element of the bill?

(c)   What efforts have been made to ensure the amount of time made available for parliamentary scrutiny has been maximised?

(d)   To what extent have interested parties and outside groups been given an opportunity to influence the policy proposal?

(e)   Does the bill include a sunset clause (as well as any appropriate renewal procedure)? If not, why does the government judge that their inclusion is not appropriate?

(f)   Are mechanisms for effective post-legislative scrutiny and review in place? If not, why does the government judge that their inclusion is not appropriate?

(g)   Has an assessment been made as to whether existing legislation is sufficient to deal with any or all of the issues in question?

(h)   Have relevant parliamentary committees been given the opportunity to scrutinise the legislation?' [331]

We recommend that this ministerial statement should be given to the Legislative Standards Committee as part of the supporting documentation provided on introduction of a bill in order that it can determine whether or not the legislation concerned meets the criteria required to be advanced on a fast-track timetable.

Greater flexibility in the timetabling of debate in the House of Commons should also be introduced in order to provide as much

---

[331]   *Ibid.*, pp.43-44.

opportunity for consideration of a fast-track bill as possible. On Mondays and Tuesdays, when the House does not start sitting until 2.30pm, business should commence earlier to allow for additional scrutiny, and while late-night sittings are unwelcome in the general operation of Parliament, in situations where time for scrutiny is so constricted, debates past 10pm would also allow for more scrutiny.

As an additional safeguard 'sunset clauses' should be included in any legislation subjected to a fast-track procedure. A sunset clause would fix an expiry date for the legislation, at which point Parliament would be required to approve the law again, if required, with more time for scrutiny. The Anti-Terrorism, Crime and Security Act 2001 provides a model in this area as a number of safeguards were incorporated into it at a late stage of its passage particularly in response to the decision to derogate in part from the Human Rights Act 1998. One safeguard was a sunset clause that provided that part of the Act would cease to operate in November 2006. Part 4 of the Act concerning the controversial detention provisions was also subject to a separate annual renewal requirement by affirmative resolution of each House. Finally a third safeguard was introduced through the provision that the entire Act would be subject to review by a committee consisting of no fewer than seven Privy Councillors who should report to Parliament no later than two years after the Act was passed. [332]

However, **whether sunset clauses are included or not, full post-legislative review should be mandatory for fast-track legislation.** A joint committee to review fast-track legislation, composed of members of both Houses, should be established with the responsibility to review emergency legislation at an agreed date after Royal Assent and with a remit to determine whether or not the legislation had sufficient constitutional and policy implications to justify being referred back to Parliament for further consideration. Given the relatively small amount of fast-track legislation that passes through Parliament each year, this would not impose a substantial additional burden of work but would improve the scrutiny function. In the interests of accountability and transparency the Government should also be required to report to the Committee, setting out its view on issues such as whether the legislation had met the government's aims, whether it had unintended consequences that were not foreseen at the time of its passage through Parliament, and what lessons had been learnt from the process.

---

[332] A. Brazier (2005), *Issues in Law Making 6: Post-Legislative Scrutiny* (London: Hansard Society), p.4.

Legislative process reforms

If better law is to be made in the future then new mechanisms to improve legislative outcomes – such as a Legislative Standards Committee and a Business Committee – are necessary. But refinements to existing processes and procedures would also greatly contribute to making better law. Parliament has many existing tools at its disposal for this purpose but often under-utilises them. By making the most of these existing procedures and utilising all the stages of scrutiny as effectively as possible in unison (thus approaching reform of the scrutiny process in a joined-up rather than the current *ad hoc* way) it should be possible to enhance the quality of law that emerges.

i) Pre-legislative scrutiny

Before a government bill is published in final form it may be published in draft as a command paper and referred to a departmental select committee for consideration. Alternatively, if a suitable departmental committee is not available, a temporary committee, for example a joint committee of both Houses, may be established.

Pre-legislative scrutiny of draft bills builds upon the long-standing practice of select committees holding inquiries into green or white papers which contain government proposals for legislative action before they are drafted into bills. This is essentially a less formal stage of pre-legislative scrutiny and it still remains an important method to allow parliamentarians to make recommendations about government plans at an early stage when the government may be more amenable to making changes. For example, in 2006 the Work and Pensions Select Committee held an inquiry into the green paper [333] that preceded the Welfare Reform Bill and made recommendations for change, some of which were accepted by the government. [334]

However, there are clear advantages in having committee consideration of the draft bill as well, for at this stage the consultation and policy deliberation is

---

[333] Department for Work and Pensions (2006), *'A new deal for welfare: Empowering people to work'*, Cm 6730.

[334] Work and Pensions Select Committee (2005-06), *'Incapacity benefits and pathways to work'*, HC 616; Department for Work and Pensions (2005-06), *Report on incapacity benefits and pathways to work, Reply by the Government to the third report of the Work and Pensions Select Committee, Session 2005-06* (HC 616), Cm 6861.

complete and the policy has been given legal expression. The purpose of pre-legislative scrutiny is to 'allow for more measured consideration of a bill's principles, questioning of new policy initiatives contained within it and consideration of any practical and technical issues which might arise from the proposed provisions'. [335] The process enables key issues to be highlighted, the subsequent debate to be framed, and technical improvements to be made to a bill. [336] More broadly, the process is helpful in stimulating public and media debate on the subject and provides a useful mechanism for external campaign and pressure groups to make their case. It is an advisory form of scrutiny only and the government remains free to accept or reject the committee's recommendations. The timing of it is such, however, that culturally ministers are more willing to make changes to it than they are at later stages when they have committed themselves to a formal bill.

From the perspective of making better law the procedure has some weaknesses: decisions about which bills should be considered in draft are made, for example, solely by the executive. Often, a draft bill is only an outline of legislative intentions setting out the framework of powers and provisions. The real detail – which will have the most impact – is contained in the regulations or delegated legislation that will later accompany it. Generally, however, these regulations are not made available at the draft stage and therefore members are able to scrutinise only a partial legislative picture. There is also a danger of overburdening select committees with work – and investigatory work in the form of policy or operational inquiries thereby taking a back seat to consideration of draft legislative proposals – although this might be offset by referring the draft bill to a joint committee. On balance, however, it is generally regarded as a beneficial process. It is difficult to be absolutely definitive about the exact influence pre-legislative scrutiny has on the emergent quality of the final bill – not least because there are no agreed criteria against which to judge this – but our previous research has found that bills have been significantly altered during the process and participants think it is a valuable stage in the legislative process. For example, the Financial Services and Markets Bill, Civil Contingencies Bill, Freedom of Information Bill, Charities Bill, and Communications Bill were all heavily influenced by pre-legislative scrutiny,

---

[335] A. Brazier (2004), *Issues in Law Making 5: Pre-legislative Scrutiny* (London: Hansard Society), p.2.

[336] G. Power (2000), *Parliamentary Scrutiny of Draft Legislation: 1997-1999* (London: Constitution Unit).

and the Corruption Bill was killed off altogether by it. [337] In certain instances it can also be particularly helpful to government for a draft bill provides a useful 'consolation prize' to a department if there is no room in the main legislative programme for a formal bill. [338]

Despite being endorsed by the Modernisation Committee in 1997, only a minority of bills were subsequently published in draft and not all were considered by committee. [339] In 2003, the government gave a tentative promise 'to proceed on the presumption that bills will be published in draft for pre-legislative scrutiny unless there is good reason otherwise', and there was a brief increase in the number of draft bills, but it soon fell back to earlier levels. [340] The House of Lords Constitution Committee's 2004 report on the legislative process recommended that pre-legislative scrutiny of draft bills should become more widespread and that the government further increase the proportion of legislation published in draft. [341] It also suggested that MPs who served on pre-legislative committees should be invited to sit at the later standing committee stage, allowing them to bring the experience gained at that earlier stage to the committee. These proposals were reiterated in the Modernisation Committee's second report on the legislative process in 2006 which strongly endorsed the value of pre-legislative scrutiny and urged its widespread use. [342]

Pre-legislative scrutiny has expanded over the last decade but not enough to become commonplace and consequently the benefits of the process have never been fully realised. Between the 1997-98 and 2003-04 parliamentary sessions, 42 bills were published in draft: in the 2003-04 parliamentary session alone, 12 draft bills were published. However, in subsequent sessions there has been a marked decline. In the 2008-09 session, for example, seven draft bills were announced but only two were then published in time for scrutiny during the session. And though the scope of pre-legislative scrutiny has been expanded to incorporate the

---

337 A. Brazier, S. Kalitowski & G. Rosenblatt with M. Korris (2008), *Law in the Making: Influence and Change in the Legislative Process* (London: Hansard Society), p.197.

338 A. Brazier (2004), *Issues in Law Making 5: Pre-legislative Scrutiny* (London: Hansard Society), p.3.

339 See Appendix V.

340 Ben Bradshaw MP, *Hansard*, 4 February 2003, col. 134W.

341 House of Lords Constitution Committee (2003-04), *Parliament and the Legislative Process*, HL 173.

342 Select Committee on the Modernisation of the House of Commons (2005-06), *The Legislative Process*, HC 1097.

Queen's Speech, of the 23 bills announced in the first-ever draft programme in July 2007, only one bill was then subsequently published in draft (the draft Constitutional Renewal Bill) and referred for full pre-legislative scrutiny to a parliamentary committee. As Alex Brazier concluded, and our seminar participants confirmed, 'Pre-legislative scrutiny has tended to be carried out on uncontroversial bills (at least those bills considered uncontroversial in party political terms).' [343] So what could be done to improve and better embed the culture of pre-legislative scrutiny within the processes of both government and Parliament?

Bills that have been subject to pre-legislative scrutiny, if conducted well, ought to need less amendment during the formal legislative process. **There is thus a case in some circumstances for bills that have been subject to pre-legislative scrutiny (or those carried-over after substantial consideration in the previous parliamentary session) to be given an accelerated passage** through the rest of the legislative process, thus freeing up more time for the scrutiny of other, more contentious, bills. If such provision were to be made, the decision should be made by the Business Committee on a case-by-case basis.

Pre-legislative scrutiny by parliamentary committee ought to be the norm for most bills. Where possible, **MPs who take part in pre-legislative scrutiny should also subsequently become members of the public bill committee** thereby ensuring that specialist knowledge of the legislation at draft stage is carried over into formal consideration of the final bill. At the very least, there should be a target that each public bill committee should have a minimum number of members who undertook pre-legislative scrutiny.

All bills which are subject to carry-over from one parliamentary session to another should have had pre-legislative scrutiny in draft form. Thus the advantages gained by the executive in securing greater flexibility in the timetabling and passage of the legislation would be balanced out by greater parliamentary scrutiny of the bill. Finally, as much as possible, **draft bills should be accompanied by a comprehensive set of draft secondary legislation** as it is these regulations that generally provide the substantive detail of a bill.

Pre-legislative scrutiny is not without its challenges but overall the potential benefits to be secured from systemic consideration of legislation in draft

---

[343] A. Brazier (2004), *Issues in Law Making 5: Pre-legislative scrutiny* (London: Hansard Society), p.4.

outweigh the problems – for example, time constraints and the additional burden of work on select committees – many of which can be addressed by other procedural reforms to streamline the legislative process.

ii) Public Bill Committee stage

In the House of Commons Modernisation Committee's 2006 report on the legislative process, the committee stage was considered and found wanting; the committee asserted that 'the work of standing committees has been one of the most criticised aspects of the legislative process', and recommended major changes to improve scrutiny. [344]

The committee recommended the replacement of standing committees with public bill committees (PBCs), to enable the taking of written and oral evidence before the examination and amendment of the bill itself. These changes were approved and adopted by the House of Commons on 1 November 2006, leading to the introduction of PBCs from January 2007.

The observations on PBCs so far have been largely positive, both from parliamentarians and external stakeholders. They appear to have improved the involvement of backbench members in committee, and the appearance of expert witnesses before PBCs has increased the quality and quantity of information available to committee members. [345] It was hoped that PBCs would be less partisan and more consensual in approach than their predecessor standing committees but in general that has not been the result. PBCs remain a forum for adversarial scrutiny and challenge. Crucially, the introduction of PBCs has also not solved the extant problems around timing that existed within standing committees, and their operation has given rise to additional issues that suggest aspects of their operation need improvement.

There is clear evidence that, although programming bites less harshly at PBC stage than at the later report stage, more time still needs to be given to committees and programming needs to be more flexible around them. At

---

[344] Select Committee on the Modernisation of the House of Commons (2005-06), *The Legislative Process*, HC 1097, p.23.

[345] For an assessment of Public Bill Committees see J. Levy (2009), *Strengthening Parliament's Powers of Scrutiny? An assessment of the introduction of Public Bill Committees* (London: Constitution Unit, University College London); A. Brazier, S. Kalitowski & G. Rosenblatt with M. Korris (2008), *Law in the Making: Influence and Change in the Legislative Process* (London: Hansard Society), pp.221-224.

present the time allocated to PBCs pays little or no heed to the size or complexity of the bill to be examined. The programme motion to set up a bill committee is moved immediately after second reading debate, with a first meeting for the committee scheduled usually only a week or two later. Both aspects of this timing arrangement potentially militate against good scrutiny. By moving the programme motion immediately after second reading, no assessment can be taken of the response of the House of Commons to the second reading debate and the issues that are likely to arise in committee. The Procedure Committee in its 2004 report recommended that the initial programme motion for a bill should not be taken less than 48 hours after second reading, to allow the proposed date for the end of committee stage to take account of the second reading debate and any representations received. [346] This would reduce the incidence of the foreshortening of debate in committee – which leads to clauses going undebated – but may also save time when more consensus is apparent at second reading than had been expected.

That clauses go undebated during PBCs is of significant concern, and it is not uncommon. Given the lack of time for scrutiny at report stage (outlined below), committee stage is the only time when thorough discussion and amendment of every clause of a bill can take place. One solution, as noted above, would be to **delay moving the programme motion to allow for a better assessment of the needs of the PBC to be made on the basis of the second reading debate**. Another option would be to introduce greater flexibility in the programming of PBCs. We have in the past recommended **the inclusion of an 'injury time' provision, to allow extra time at the end of a PBC to return to clauses where debate was cut short**. [347]

Another useful reform would be to regularly **use split committals on bills**. A split committal involves debating some sections of a bill (usually those clauses containing the most controversial aspects) on the floor of the House of Commons, while allowing the less controversial or more technical elements to be considered in PBC. The facility to do this exists under Standing Order 63(3) but is rarely used at Westminster (the process is more commonly utilised in the Scottish Parliament). This would potentially make the programming of PBCs more predictable and compensate for some of the shortcomings of report stage, as the Commons as

---

[346] House of Commons Procedure Committee (2003-04), *Programming of Legislation*, HC 325, p.10.

[347] A. Brazier (ed) (2004), *Parliament, Politics and Law Making: Issues & Developments in the Legislative Process* (London: Hansard Society), p.27.

a whole would get two opportunities to debate and amend controversial elements. It would also have the additional value of involving principal frontbenchers in the debate at committee stage as they currently rarely serve on PBCs. As a consequence, the increased political pressure on report stage – because that is where the key front-benchers now meet head to head – might also be relieved. **Under the current system, the 'usual channels' would identify the most controversial areas of the bill – both the points of contention between the government and opposition and between the government and its own backbenchers – and split the bill accordingly. Under our reform proposals, the House Business Committee would oversee the splitting of the bill.** It would enable MPs to prioritise those issues they most want to concentrate on, and avoid the unnecessary double-handling of all aspects of a bill.

PBCs also need significantly more time built into their operation if the evidence-gathering sessions are to function adequately. There is often insufficient time between the end of second reading and the commencement of a PBC to allow members of the committee to meet to consider the witnesses they wish to call, and so the decision is taken by the 'usual channels'; a design flaw that leads to the 'usual suspects' often being invited to give evidence. [348]

The restricted time allowed around PBCs also causes difficulties for witnesses. In the case of the Counter-Terrorism Bill Committee, some witnesses were only given 24 hours' notice of being asked to give evidence. [349] This is compounded by the fact that the clerks do not have sufficient time to prepare briefings for members of the committee, potentially reducing the quality of scrutiny.

The programming of the evidence-gathering sessions themselves is also a concern, as a set amount of time is fixed in advance to take evidence from each witness. This is in contrast to select committees where there is flexibility to over-run if members still wish to question an interesting witness, or to cut short a session if all useful angles of scrutiny have been exhausted. **We recommend that during sittings where multiple witnesses are scheduled, it be left to the discretion of the chair as to the management of time. Programme motions should be amended as required to allow this.** [350]

---

[348] A. Brazier, S. Kalitowski & G. Rosenblatt with M. Korris (2008), *Law in the Making: Influence and Change in the Legislative Process* (London: Hansard Society), p.223.

[349] *Ibid.*

[350] *Ibid.*, pp.222-223.

Chairs rather than Whips should be invested with the power to call the witnesses. Overall, there is considerable scope to improve the chairing of PBCs in order to enhance their effectiveness. **A review of chairing arrangements should be undertaken** with a view to facilitating improvements, for example through greater involvement of select committee chairs or a more enhanced role for members of the Chairmen's Panel supported by greater assistance and briefing from clerks.

Given the complexity of legislation, experts, lawyers and even officials should also be able to speak at PBCs – not to be part of the debate but to provide clarification or explanation in order to assist members in undertaking forensic scrutiny during this crucial part of the legislative process.

More time is also required between the evidence-gathering phase of a PBC and the line-by-line consideration of the bill. Edward Garnier MP highlighted the problem at the start of the PBC considering the 2007 Criminal Justice and Immigration Bill: 'I have some private doubts as to the usefulness of the arrangement – I say that these are private doubts because we are in Committee, so no one is listening – because the Public Bill Committee starts next week and there is, therefore, very little time between the closing of the evidence sessions on Thursday and the beginning of the Committee on Tuesday, for the Government to do anything about the evidence that they have received'. [351]

Both government and opposition members of the PBC need sufficient time to examine and reflect on the evidence presented, and to draft appropriate amendments to the bill. **There should be the expectation of one sitting week at the very least between the two stages of the PBC** to allow this to happen.

Written evidence is permitted for all PBCs but oral evidence cannot be taken for any bill originating in the House of Lords or which has not been subject to pre-legislative scrutiny. These are unhelpful restrictions: **the House of Lords should reform their procedures to establish public evidence hearings for bills that originate in the Upper House** and **where pre-legislative scrutiny has taken place this should be the starting point for**

---

[351] Edward Garnier MP, Criminal Justice and Immigration Bill, 1st sitting, 16 October 2007, col. 5.

examination by the PBC, regardless of where the bill originated, a position previously recommended by the Modernisation Committee. [352]

iii) Report stage

Report stage was described by the Wright Committee as 'the single greatest cause of dissatisfaction which we have detected with current scheduling of legislative business'. [353] It is regularly hobbled by a lack of time for debate with one, or very occasionally two, days of debate often being insufficient to allow for thorough scrutiny of the work of the PBC. This stage has consequently been described as 'useless' and 'in need of a lot of work' by opposition frontbenchers, although there is recognition of its importance as the one opportunity when all members of the House of Commons can get involved in the detailed amendment of bills. [354]

The problem of time is exacerbated by the government's propensity to radically amend and add new clauses to a bill at this stage. For example, the Legislative and Regulatory Reform Bill 2006 was so heavily amended by government at report stage that no time was available to discuss parts two and three of the bill.[355] Similarly, the Criminal Justice and Immigration Bill 2007 and the Planning Bill 2008 were both subject to a substantial amount of government amendment at report stage, which dramatically undermined the quality of scrutiny that the Commons could bring to bear.

While report stage cannot provide time for debate on every clause and amendment, it is clear that more time is required if it is going to adequately fulfil its purpose. A minimum standard should be set for debating the entirety of the bill and a certain proportion of well-supported amendments. Programme motions are often amended at report stage, but this is rarely to add sufficient time for scrutiny in the eyes of opposition parties, and they are regularly pressed to division. However, speakers are acutely aware that the time spent

---

[352] Select Committee on the Modernisation of the House of Commons (2005-06), *The Legislative Process*, HC 1097.

[353] Reform of the House of Commons Committee (2008-09), *Rebuilding the House*, HC 1117, p.35.

[354] A. Brazier, S. Kalitowski & G. Rosenblatt with M. Korris (2008), *Law in the Making: Influence and Change in the Legislative Process* (London: Hansard Society), p.120.

[355] *Ibid.*, p.223.

debating and dividing on the programme motion further reduces the time available for scrutiny. **It would therefore be beneficial if programme motions were moved separately to report stage – a day or two in advance – to ensure that debate on those motions does not cut into the time available for scrutiny of the bill itself.**

And **if government tables such a significant number of amendments at this stage that it substantially alters the nature of the bill, the Business Committee should be able to facilitate its recommittal** (return it to committee stage). In the meantime, the Speaker might be given this power. Additionally, **if the government tables amendments to its own bill it should have to explain the reasons for doing so by way of an explanatory statement.** It would then become possible over time to discern whether the number of amendments being made are as a result of the government's own failings in relation to, for example, late policy changes or poor preparation and drafting, or in response to ideas that have emerged during the scrutiny process or commitments given by ministers at PBC stage. Over time, the explanation for the volume of amendments will thus become much clearer and, following review, further ameliorating reforms either pre-introduction in Whitehall, or post-introduction in Parliament can be made where appropriate.

iv) Third reading

Third reading debates are intended to consider the revised shape of the bill, following its amendment at committee and report stages before it is passed to the other House to consider. However, in the House of Commons, short third readings are often squeezed in at the end of report stage, as part of a 'remaining stages' day of debate.

While there is little in the way of surplus time in the legislative process, there is a strong case for having a full third reading debate given the weaknesses of report stage as outlined above. It would be advantageous to maintain some flexibility around the use of third reading debates. **Where a bill has been heavily amended – in PBC or especially by the government at report stage – a full third reading should take place.** Where change has been minor or consensus exists, the need for a third reading is obviated. The PBC itself could make a recommendation at the end of its sitting as to whether it considered a third reading might be necessary. In time, this decision should be made by a Business Committee; in the interim, it will be for the parties via the 'usual channels', and therefore the government in particular, to commit itself to adopt this reform.

v) A new Legislative Committee system?

A more radical change to improve the legislative process would be to formally involve select committees in the scrutiny of legislation through a new Legislative Committee system combining the membership of select committees and PBCs into one Legislative Committee process. A long-standing criticism of committee stage at Westminster is that the expertise built up by select committees is not sufficiently utilised in the legislative scrutiny process and there is well-founded suspicion that the whips prevent members with interest and expertise from joining committees where their knowledge could be effectively deployed if they suspect they will not be entirely loyal. [356]

While currently select committees may choose to examine bills that come forward, they are not required to and – importantly – the legislative process will not wait for them to do so. This causes complaints from committees who argue they are being denied the opportunity to contribute properly to the legislation – recent examples being the House of Commons Political and Constitutional Reform Committee in relation to the Parliamentary Voting System and Constituencies Bill [357] and the House of Lords Constitution Committee in relation to the Public Bodies Bill. [358]

Here, Westminster might learn from the experience of committee scrutiny processes in both the Scottish Parliament and the National Assembly for Wales. Both models have notable advantages for legislative scrutiny, particularly in utilising the expertise of members in a subject area, although both have significant implications in terms of the demands placed on the resources of committees and the time of parliamentarians.

---

[356] *Ibid.*, p.200.

[357] House of Commons Political and Constitutional Reform Committee (2010-11), *Parliamentary Voting System and Constituencies Bill*, HC 422.

[358] House of Lords Constitution Committee (2010-11), *Public Bodies Bill [HL]*, HL 51.

a) Committee scrutiny in Scotland

Parliamentary committees in Scotland play a central role in the legislative scrutiny process, with all public bills initially sent to the relevant subject committee (or committees) for consideration of their general principles and, if approved, for further debate and amendment. [359] Committees may also undertake a form of pre-legislative scrutiny, although this is usually an early preparation and familiarisation for Stage One scrutiny rather than a distinctly separate process involving the publication of a report. At Holyrood, pre-legislative scrutiny 'is not viewed as a mechanism through which to seek changes to government legislation before it is introduced'.[360] Stage One for all executive (and members') bills is consideration by the relevant committee of the principles of the bill. If the subject of the bill covers the remit of more than one committee, then the Parliamentary Bureau [361] will nominate a 'lead committee' to undertake the task, though 'secondary committees' can report on the bill to the lead committee. This often includes the Subordinate Legislation Committee that deals with delegated legislation.

The lead committee will take evidence on the bill in a similar way to a Westminster select committee by requesting written and oral evidence, usually including a hearing with the responsible minister. The committee will then publish a report on its findings, highlighting any concerns it has on the general principles of the bill and usually making a recommendation as to whether the bill should proceed or not. The committee also comments on the extent of the consultation undertaken and whether further evidence should be collected to inform the next stage of consideration of the bill. [362] The conclusion of Stage One scrutiny will then be a plenary debate on the findings of the report and a vote on whether the bill should be allowed to proceed to Stage Two.

---

[359] See Appendix III for a diagram of the legislative process in the Scottish Parliament.

[360] J. Johnston, 'The Legislative Process: The Parliament in Practice' in C. Jeffery and J. Mitchell (eds) (2009), *The Scottish Parliament 1999-2009: The First Decade* (Edinburgh: Luath Press), p.31.

[361] The equivalent of a House Business Committee, this body organises the parliament's programme of business and the arrangements of parliamentary committees. Its members include the Presiding Officer and a representative from each political party which has five or more MSPs and a representative of any grouping of five or more members from parties with fewer than five MSPs or from no political party.

[362] D. Arter (2002), 'On Assessing Strength and Weakness in Parliamentary Committee Systems: Some Preliminary Observations on the New Scottish Parliament', *Journal of Legislative Studies*, 8(2), pp.93-117.

For Stage Two consideration the bill returns to the lead committee, unless a motion is passed to nominate an alternative committee or consideration takes place on the floor of the Chamber (Committee of the Whole House).[363] The Stage Two committee process considers the text of the bill in detail in much the same format as PBCs at Westminster, with the option of taking further evidence dependent on the timescale available and the recommendations from the Stage One committee report. While it is not usual for a Stage Two committee to produce a separate report alongside the amended version of the bill, it has the option of doing so, to explain why particular amendments were made or to draw the Parliament's attention to provisions of the bill where, although the committee could not agree on any particular amendments, it agrees that some amendment is required.

The advantage of this Scottish model is that there is an expectation built into the system that the same committee will be involved in both Stage One and Two scrutiny, enabling expertise and experience to be carried through from one stage to the next. It may also result in less repetition of arguments if the participants remain the same throughout; a particular problem at Westminster given the differing membership of committees considering bills at the pre-legislative and PBC stages. The production of a detailed report at Stage One also helps to inform and enhance debate in the plenary sessions that follow.

There are some disadvantages however. The Parliament's Committee Convenors Group (the equivalent of the Liaison Committee in Westminster) has registered some concern that the legislative aspect of committee work dominates to the detriment of other important aspects of committee work, particularly inquiries. In a report at the end of the second session it noted that this 'creates the possibility that scrutiny through inquiries will not be as rigorous as it should be. It also gives rise to the possibility that poor legislation will be enacted without proper detailed scrutiny.'[364] The Convenors Group has also expressed concern that committee remits or ministerial portfolios have been adjusted to allow referral of bills to committees 'whose work programme could better accommodate them but which had no previous background or

---

[363] The Parliamentary Bureau may also propose that the bill be divided among two or more committees for Stage Two consideration – preferably with each committee being allocated whole Parts or Chapters to deal with.

[364] Scottish Parliament Committee Conveners' Group (2007), *Legacy Paper – Second Session*, http://www.scottish.parliament.uk/s3/committees/committeeConvenersGroup/docs/LegacyPaperSession2.pdf.

experience in the subject matter'. It concluded that the Scottish Government was deliberately deploying this 'artificial device' to ensure its bills could proceed as it wished, in contravention of the founding idea that the committees were meant to develop knowledge and expertise in a policy area in order to provide more effective scrutiny. [365]

While the number of committees in Westminster is greater, and therefore the burden of legislative scrutiny would likely be reduced through a more efficient distribution, if this combination Legislative Committee model were to be used, there would still be risks that it would undermine the other scrutiny functions undertaken by select committees. Adopting such a procedure would therefore need to be undertaken in the context of a significant review of the workings of select committees, with possible emphasis on a greater use of sub-committees and a commensurate increase in resources.

b) Committee scrutiny in Wales

Committees also play a central role in the scrutiny of legislation in the Welsh Assembly. The Government for Wales Act 2006 enables the National Assembly for Wales to seek legislative competence, via the Orders in Council procedure or via Westminster bills. Once legislative competence is granted, the Assembly can then make laws for Wales, called Assembly Measures, which represent the Welsh equivalent of Acts of Parliament.

Legislative scrutiny of Measures by committees is similar to that of bills in the Scottish Parliament, in that Stage One is committee consideration of the principles of the legislation, followed by a plenary debate to consider the findings of the committee, and then Stage Two is committee consideration where amendments may be moved. [366] Where the process differs from Scotland is that the legislation committees in Wales are separate from the subject committees, and like PBCs at Westminster they have no policy focus or specialisation (although one committee is dedicated entirely to dealing with member-proposed legislation).

Unlike Westminster however, the legislation committees have a permanent membership, though in practice members are often substituted in and out on

---

[365] *Ibid.*

[366] A diagram of the legislative process in Wales in provided in Appendix III.

a regular basis. This in part reflects the burden of committee work in a small Chamber, as there are effectively around 45 Assembly Members to cover the work of approximately 18 permanent committees. [367] However, it allows members with an interest in the topic to find a place on committees considering relevant pieces of legislation, and it often results in members of the relevant subject committee coming in to scrutinise legislation in that area. For example, while scrutinising the Children and Families Measure (2009), four out of the six members of Legislation Committee No. 2 were also members of the Enterprise and Learning Committee or the Children and Young People Committee. Similarly, the membership of the Legislation Committee No. 1, while scrutinising the Playing Fields Measure (2008), included four Assembly Members (out of six) from the Children and Young People, Enterprise and Learning or Health, Wellbeing and Local Government Committees. Cross-pollination of scrutiny resources happens naturally due to the structural and operational features of the Assembly, rather than it being a deliberately contrived process. While this transfer of members in and out of the permanent legislation committees prevents any committee from developing expertise as a body, the utilisation of members with relevant experience from other committees makes up for this loss.

Bearing in mind the lessons to be learnt from both devolved legislature models, **we recommend that the House of Commons should review its committee system with a view to trialling the introduction of several Legislative Committees for the remainder of this Parliament. These committees would seek, as far as possible, to combine the membership of departmental select committees and PBCs for consideration of those bills that receive pre-legislative scrutiny.**

vi) Post-legislative scrutiny

Ensuring that the implementation of legislation has been effective is an important task in the context of making better law but it is one that has long been neglected by Parliament. As the Hansard Society noted in a previous study of post-legislative scrutiny, 'Once a law is enacted and implemented, its provisions bind society, unless it is subsequently repealed or amended.

---

[367] The National Assembly for Wales has 60 members, but the Presiding Officer and the Welsh Assembly Government members do not take part in committee legislative scrutiny.

Yet it is often only after its implementation that the effects and implications of an Act can be truly assessed. However, it is also at this point that Parliament usually shifts its focus to other measures that require scrutiny and authorisation.' [368] There is of course little incentive for government to devote further time, resources, and political capital to revisit an area of policy and legislation in order, ostensibly, to discover where it may have been less than successful. And, given the existing scrutiny and resource pressures facing Parliament due to the torrent of legislation it must consider, there has been little pressure at Westminster to push the importance of this area of scrutiny work.

However, it would be a mistake to consider post-legislative scrutiny purely through a prism of determining mistakes and apportioning blame. If this form of scrutiny continues to be *ad hoc* then inevitably it will focus on those areas of legislation that prompt controversy or which have palpably failed to meet their intended objectives. Regular post-legislative review of most Acts some years after implementation should uncover both good and bad practice, assessing whether legislation has fulfilled its intended purpose, and if not what alternative measures might be needed to achieve the desired goal. It would provide a useful check to ensure that the measures set out in the Act are indeed being implemented in the manner and by whom it was intended. At its best, post-legislative scrutiny would help to improve current and future law by fostering a culture of learning and development within government departments and Parliament.

Select committees have chosen to conduct inquiries into the effects of legislation within their remit for many years, especially if there is a public, parliamentary or media concern about the Act in question. But the current *ad hoc* approach to post-legislative scrutiny, although valuable for what it may reveal about specific pieces of legislation, is insufficiently embedded into formal procedures in Westminster and Whitehall to truly make an impact. The value of the process is not being sufficiently leveraged. In the 2008-09 parliamentary session for example, the Commons Culture, Media and Sport Select Committee reviewed the operation of the 2003 Licensing Act at its own initiative. This legislation brought together a range of other Acts covering different types of licensing to create a uniform system of regulation for the

---

[368] A. Brazier (2005), *Issues in Law Making 6: Post-Legislative Scrutiny* (London: Hansard Society), p.1.

provision of alcohol, regulated entertainment and the provision of late night refreshment. [369] There had been much controversy in particular about the impact of this new licensing regime on small music venues and the government had at the time undertaken to review its operation after 6-12 months of operation. In March 2008 the government duly published the findings of its review. [370] This indicated that some parts of the legislation were more successful than others. On the positive side, the new local authority alcohol licensing was deemed to be successful and the police, local authorities and other bodies were working better in partnership. [371] However, the report noted that the overall impact on crime was neutral and there was some evidence of displacement of crime to the early hours. [372] This led the government to make a number of amendments to policy and the report indicated a range of planned changes to legislation including increasing the maximum fine for a person refusing to stop drinking or give up their drink in a designated area from £500 to £2,500. [373]

As a result of its own inquiries, the select committee made a range of further recommendations including establishing a national database of personal licence holders, and clarifying the legal changes to the temporary Events Notice provisions to increase the power to object, while increasing the numbers of Notices that an individual can apply for annually to 15. However, the government chose not to accept any of the committee's recommendations. It advised that it was consulting on or considering some of the matters raised by the committee [374] and on a number of issues agreed on the importance of clear guidance, but did not accept the recommendations that the existing guidance should be amended. [375] The process was not completely without value, for

---

[369] Licensing Act 2003 (as enacted), Explanatory Notes at para.6.

[370] Department for Culture, Media and Sport (2008), *Evaluation of the Impact of the Licensing Act 2003*.

[371] *Ibid.*, p.7.

[372] *Ibid.*, p.8.

[373] *Ibid.*, p.10-11.

[374] This included an extension of the time for bereaved families dealing with a licence and an extension of the time for objections to an application for a Temporary Event Notice. Department for Culture, Media and Sport (2008), *Government Response to the House of Commons Culture, Media and Sport Select Committee on the Licensing Act 2003*, Cm 7684, p.3 & pp.8-9.

[375] E.g. clearer guidance on licensing conditions. Department for Culture, Media and Sport (2008), *Government Response to the House of Commons Culture, Media and Sport Select Committee on the Licensing Act 2003*, Cm 7684, p.8.

reference has been made to the committee's recommendations in other debates in the years since. In 2009, for example, during passage in the House of Lords of the Policing and Crime Bill 2009, which amended the licensing regime for lap-dancing clubs, a reference was made to the select committee's recommendation regarding extension of the licensing period for these clubs. [376] Again, the government re-iterated that it did not accept the need for change but the existence of the report enabled members to continue to press the government and provided an evidence base against which to test the government's latest proposals. But if post-legislative review was pursued in a more systematic way, then more value could be extracted from the process in the interests of both the government and Parliament.

The case for some form of post-legislative review was made by the House of Commons Procedure Committee twice during the 1970s and again in 1990. In 1993 the Hansard Society Commission on the Legislative Process argued that all Acts of Parliament (with the exception of Finance Acts and constitutional legislation) should be reviewed two or three years after they come into force. [377] In 1997 the Modernisation Committee argued that 'Monitoring and, if necessary, amending legislation which has come into force should become a vital part of the role of Parliament.' [378] The idea received support in 2001 from Robin Cook MP as Leader of the House of Commons [379] and in 2002 the Liaison Committee agreed that one of the core tasks of select committees should be to 'examine the implementation of legislation and major policy initiatives'. [380] However, no system of post-legislative scrutiny was established at that time, and only sporadically were any acts examined for their effects. The House of Lords Constitution Committee concluded in 2004 that 'Post-legislative scrutiny appears to be similar to motherhood and apple pie in that everyone appears to be in favour of it. However, unlike motherhood and apple pie, it is not much in evidence.' [381]

---

[376] Baroness Hanham, *Hansard*, 6 July 2009, vol. 712 col. 514.

[377] Hansard Society (1993), *Making the Law, The Report of the Hansard Society Commission on the Legislative Process* (London: Hansard Society), p.95.

[378] Select Committee on Modernisation of the House of Commons (1997-98), *The Legislative Process*, HC 190, para.14.

[379] Select Committee on Modernisation of the House of Commons (2001-02), *Modernisation of the House of Commons: A Reform Programme for Consultation – Memorandum submitted by the Leader of the House of Commons*.

[380] House of Commons Liaison Committee (2002-03), *Annual Report for 2002*, HC 558, p.9.

[381] House of Lords Constitution Committee (2003-04), *Parliament and the Legislative Process*, HL 173, p.42.

In 2006 the Law Commission undertook a consultation to examine the options for parliamentary post-legislative scrutiny, and alternatives such as its own review processes. [382] It recommended the establishment of a Joint Committee on Post-Legislative Scrutiny, with a remit to consider both bills and Acts to decide whether they are suitable for post-legislative scrutiny by Parliament, though it rejected a formal fixed timetable for the review of all primary legislation. [383] In 2008 the government published its response, setting out a system for post-legislative scrutiny under which the department responsible for an Act would produce a memorandum three to five years after Royal Assent, for scrutiny by the relevant select committee (or, if appropriate, a joint committee). This would cover matters including:

- an indication of any specific legal or drafting difficulties which had been matters of public concern (e.g. issues which had been the subject of actual litigation or of comment from parliamentary committees) and had been addressed;

- a summary of any other known post-legislative reviews or assessments of the Act conducted in government, by Parliament, or elsewhere; and

- a short preliminary assessment of how the Act has worked out in practice, relative to objectives and benchmarks identified at the time of the passage of the bill. [384]

In addition the government indicated that impact assessments and explanatory notes with strengthened guidance would be the basis for any post-legislative review. [385] This system was to apply to all Acts receiving Royal Assent after 2005. [386] However, while a small number of departmental

---

[382] *Ibid.*, p.9.

[383] The Law Commission (2006), *Post-Legislative Scrutiny*, LC No. 302, Cm 6945, paras 6.6-6.11.

[384] Office of the Leader of the House of Commons (2008), *Post-Legislative Scrutiny: The Government's Approach*, Cm 7320, paras 16-17.

[385] *Ibid.*, para 14.

[386] Certain Acts are exempt from the process. These are Consolidated Fund and Appropriation Acts, Finance Acts, Tax Law Rewrite Acts, Consolidation Acts, Statute Law Repeal Acts and Private Acts. Cabinet Office, *Guide to making Legislation*, para.41.10, http://www.cabinetoffice.gov.uk/making-legislation-guide/post-legislative_scrutiny.aspx.

memorandums have been published, few have yet been scrutinised by committees in Parliament. [387] The process will need to be examined in the coming years to ascertain whether the memorandums produced by the government are sufficiently relevant and detailed and what usage committees are making of them.

There exists an issue of resources for select committees undertaking the task of post-legislative scrutiny. For committees covering departments such as the Home Office, where, as set out in chapter 1, three or four bills per session are not uncommon, the additional workload to conduct post-legislative scrutiny thoroughly may impact on the committee's other important scrutiny work. However, to offset this, the expertise of members of the House of Lords could offer a great deal, particularly in areas of very technical scrutiny – such as, for example, review of audit mechanisms, departmental memoranda, regulatory and environmental impact assessments – of the kind that would be required in an effective post-legislative scrutiny process. Ideally, **a Joint Committee for Post-Legislative Review should be established to examine any legislation that the relevant departmental House of Commons select committee declines to look at**. It would sift Acts eligible for review under the three to five year rule and determine which ones or which specific aspects of the legislation it would like to review.

The committee would be empowered to take both oral and written evidence from experts, pressure groups and those directly affected by the legislation. It would also open the way to greater interaction between Parliament and the courts as a key stakeholder audience would necessarily be lawyers and the judiciary who will have had to interpret and implement the legislation, and will be in a position to debate weaknesses in the law, including any ambiguities and errors. The courts have often been critical of Parliament for not doing its job properly in terms of making the law; post-legislative scrutiny raises the intriguing prospect that Parliament might choose to put the work and function of judges and the courts under a greater microscope in relation to interpretation and implementation of certain statutes.

---

[387] Eleven post-legislative memorandums for Acts from 2005 had been published as of 18 November 2010. A further five are due before the end of 2010.

Reform of House of Lords legislative procedures [388]

Peers as much as MPs have a constitutional obligation to ensure effective scrutiny of all legislation and many members of the Upper House are greatly concerned about the standard of law currently being produced. There is, as was discussed at several of our seminars, a widely held perception, purveyed not least by many peers, that the standard of scrutiny deployed in the law-making process in the Upper House is significantly better than in the House of Commons. As one seminar participant noted, there is 'a general impression that the House of Commons sends its not very good prep up to the Lords and that it then comes back with lots of red pen all over it and *non satis* written at the end'. But for all the flaws outlined in the Commons procedures, it is open to debate as to whether the approach of peers is markedly better than MPs. The number of legislative amendments accepted in the House of Lords does not automatically equate to better standards of scrutiny. Over the last decade the government has not had a majority in the Upper House so in many instances peers have been in a better position to extract concessions on significant political issues. Previous Hansard Society research found that many amendments made by the House of Lords were in fact based on concerns that had first been raised in the Commons. [389] The House of Lords was better able to execute the change but the two Houses were working in partnership to achieve it. Ministers have been generally more willing to make concessions in the Lords because it is not under the same media spotlight as the Commons. Changes in the membership and therefore the balance of political control in the House, coupled with the impact of coalition politics, may change the approach to scrutiny in the Lords over the course of this Parliament.

MPs also have a wider range of responsibilities beyond legislative scrutiny, not least their obligations to their constituents that impose a heavy workload

---

[388] In 2009-10 the Hansard Society (Peter Riddell and Ruth Fox) provided some advisory and drafting support to a cross-party group of peers, chaired by Lord Filkin, that was set up to explore how scrutiny of primary legislation by the House of Lords might be improved. The work of this group, and two similar groups exploring non-legislative procedural reform and improved governance in the Upper House, led to the formation in the summer of 2010 of a Lords Leaders Group on the Working Practices of the House of Lords chaired by Lord Goodlad. At the time of writing it is still deliberating. The reforms outlined in this section of the report therefore draw heavily on the Hansard Society's work with the Filkin group as set out in the report of the cross-party peers group on 'Improving scrutiny of primary legislation in the House of Lords', March 2010.

[389] A. Brazier, S. Kalitowski & G. Rosenblatt with M. Korris (2008), *Law in the Making: Influence and Change in the Legislative Process* (London: Hansard Society), p.184. See also M. Russell & M. Sciara (2007), *The House of Lords in 2006: Negotiating a Stronger Second Chamber* (London: Constitution Unit).

burden on their time and resources of a kind not faced by peers. Differing perceptions of expertise are also an important facet of this debate: it is widely asserted in many quarters that peers provide more expert scrutiny than do MPs. This is certainly true, reflecting to some degree the increasingly narrow social and professional base from which MPs are currently recruited. But it is also true that the nature of an MP's role imposes limitations on their expertise. Many peers combine life as a parliamentarian with the continued development of their professional careers and therefore their expertise as academics, scientists, businessmen, surgeons etc. This is not open to MPs: the nature of a career in the Commons means that in most instances the extent of their expertise remains dated at the point at which they enter the House and thereby leave behind their previous occupational experience. MPs, however, bring to debate a front-line knowledge and experience of a wide range of different policies and laws derived from their constituency work that most peers simply cannot match.

That is why, **in the interest of making better law, both Houses should work more closely together to develop a system of scrutiny on a bi-cameral basis in which the specific expertise of the Upper House is effectively deployed to augment the scrutiny that takes place in the House of Commons.** For the House of Lords this means avoiding duplication of scrutiny work and greater co-ordination with and dovetailing of scrutiny with the House of Commons, whilst recognising that one size does not fit all and there will inevitably be some variation in the scrutiny methods used by each House.

As previously indicated, ideally both **a new Legislative Standards Committee and a Joint Committee for Post-Legislative Review should be convened on a bi-cameral basis.**

If a new Business Committee is established within three years, then the 'usual channels' will no longer operate in the same way and the House of Lords should therefore consider establishing its own Business Committee. **Some form of Joint Business Liaison mechanism must be established to enable cross-Chamber discussions to take place regarding how each House is to examine legislation** to ensure that proper scrutiny takes place at each stage in an efficient and effective manner and that the scrutiny work of each House complements and augments rather than duplicates the work of the other.

It is now an accepted aspect of making better law that the parliamentary scrutiny process benefits from the engagement of the public, both experts and interested stakeholders, in direct consideration of the legislative process. At some stage every bill should therefore be subject to a public evidence hearing as occurs in the House of Commons through the Public Bill Committee process. However, bills originating in the House of Lords are not subject to such public evidence sessions when they reach the House of Commons. If this is not changed in the Commons then **the House of Lords should adopt a public evidence hearing committee for all bills that originate in the Upper House, unless peers determine that the nature of the bill is such that the House discharges itself from that duty** (for example, if the bill has already been subject to pre-legislative scrutiny).

The bill should be referred to a temporary select committee established specifically to take evidence – oral or written – on the bill after second reading. Members of this temporary committee would be appointed in accordance with the normal appointment process to committees, and members would decide which witnesses they wished to call and the form and conduct of questioning. A distinctive feature of House of Lords procedures is the commitment to self-regulation and consensus, to ensuring fair representation of all sides in proceedings, and to the fullest participation of members without the constraints of timetabling. Reflecting this, it should be open to any member of the House to therefore attend the evidence taking proceedings and ask a question; however, only members of the select committee should deliberate and vote on any final report emerging from the evidence session on the bill. The committee's report should clearly focus on highlighting those issues that the members wish to draw to the attention of the whole House to assist them in conducting later scrutiny. The committee would not have the power to amend or delay a bill – its role would be solely to facilitate the holding of public evidence hearings and the reporting back of findings from these hearings to the rest of the House.

These same committee members should then also consider the bill at Grand Committee stage in order to ensure that the bank of knowledge about the detail of the bill generated through the temporary select committee stage can be maximised for the benefit of all members at this later stage of detailed consideration.

Facilitating this public evidence stage will require some additional time in the legislative timetable but much, if not all, of this could be offset by the time-savings that can be made through other linked reforms particularly at Grand

Committee and report stage. **Grand Committee should be the default mechanism for consideration of all bills in the Lords unless otherwise required by the House**. Greater use of Grand Committee would help to rationalise the scrutiny process and prioritise the use of time in the Chamber to best effect. In addition, as recommended for the Commons, **the House of Lords should also make greater use of the opportunity for split committal of bills with contentious issues continuing to be considered and voted on in the Chamber**. Recommendations on split committal should be made by the temporary select committee that conducts the public evidence hearings. It will be in a position to determine quickly which aspects of the bill are the most contentious and report back to the House accordingly for its consideration. If the majority of bills are dealt with in Grand Committee then **this will free up more time in the Chamber for consideration of bills at report stage**. Given current procedures, implementation of this reform will require either agreement that the House should not consider a bill at report stage after the dinner hour; or reform of the sitting hours of the House.

Finally, new mechanisms should be put in place to alert peers to those sections of a bill that have not been scrutinised in the Commons. **When a bill passes from the Commons to the Lords any clauses that have not been debated, should therefore be 'flagged' either by annotation of the Order Paper or marking-up of the bill.** This would help inform peers as to the state of scrutiny of the bill, enabling them to then determine whether and how to prioritise these hitherto un-scrutinised clauses.

Taken together this package of reforms would substantially improve the scrutiny processes in the Upper House, particularly the management of that most vital resource, namely time. They would also provide a substantial platform for the development of an effective, integrated process of bi-cameral scrutiny which should help both improve the law-making process and enable each House to derive benefits in terms of time and resource savings.

More broadly the government has said it intends to bring forward plans for next-stage reform of the composition of the House of Lords in this parliamentary session. To date, much of the debate about the future of the Lords has centred on whether members should be elected or not, and if so what the system of election used should be. This debate has thus far largely neglected the equally vital questions about exactly what role and function members of a reformed Upper House should play in the legislative scrutiny process in the future. **This debate must take place. As a revising Chamber, detailed proposals for how a reformed House of Lords will deal with legislation should be a paramount concern and priority within the reform package, not a subsidiary issue as appears too often to be the case at present.**

Delegated legislation

As outlined in chapter 1, primary legislation often provides only a framework for particular policies, leaving delegated or secondary legislation to fill in much of the detail. And, like primary legislation, the volume of SIs has increased significantly over the last quarter century. Regarded as a 'tedious corner of the constitutional edifice', most delegated legislation operates below the parliamentary and public radar. [390] However, as Page notes, far from being dull and routine, trivial or arcane, SIs constitute the process of government and provide a window on it, for they embrace every facet of life: 'We can find SIs to cover our daily lives from the alarm clock that wakes us up in the morning, the bread we eat for our breakfast, the car in which we drive to work, the roads we drive on, the contents of the herbal tea that many of us take as a nightcap, the electric switch we turn off before we go to sleep, as well as the beds we sleep on, and everything in between.' [391] Yet despite their importance and the increase in the number of regulations each year, scrutiny of them by Parliament remains wholly inadequate.

SIs are subject to one of four different forms of scrutiny, namely those:

i. that only have to be made, or laid before Parliament, to come into effect;

ii. subject to the 'negative' procedure which comes into force unless a motion to annul them (known as a prayer or praying against them) is passed within 40 sitting days;

iii. subject to the 'affirmative' procedure, which means that they cannot become law unless both Houses first approve a draft';

---

[390] J.D. Hayhurst & P. Wallington (1998), 'The Parliamentary Scrutiny of Delegated Legislation', in M. Zander (1994), *The Law Making Process* (London: Butterworths), p.95.

[391] E.C. Page (2001), *Governing by Numbers: Delegated Legislation and Every Day Policy Making* (Oxford: Hart Publishing), p.vii.

iv.   subject to the 'super-affirmative' procedure, which usually have to be preceded by proposals that are subject to public consultation.

The drafting of primary legislation clauses often confers very broad order-making powers through wording such as '*in relation to*' and '*in connection with*', the intention of which may not be fully debated, and therefore not fully clear, due to the restricted time available for scrutiny. There is therefore a real danger that wide-ranging powers can be hidden and then activated through one of the SI procedures or that such powers can be utilised in a way that was not originally intended at the time the legislation was passed (for example, the way in which the asset freezing powers contained in the Anti-Terrorism, Crime and Security Act 2001 were used to freeze the assets of the Icelandic bank, Landsbanki in 2008).

In 2003 the House of Lords established a sifting mechanism – the Merits of Statutory Instruments Committee – to determine which Statutory Instruments are of sufficient legal or political import that they merit further debate. This reform has strengthened the role of the Lords and its scrutiny function. This committee and the Delegated Powers and Regulatory Reform Committee provide an important check on delegated legislation but the effectiveness of this scrutiny function is necessarily constrained by the nature and limitations of the approval process for SIs.

The majority of SIs are subject to the 'negative' procedure which means they become law in the form determined by ministers unless either the House of Commons or the House of Lords votes against them. In practice, however, this rarely happens. Initiative lies with the opposition to table appropriate annulment motions in the form of Early Day Motions (known as 'prayers'). However, because the executive controls the use of time in the House, these are only debated if the government agrees. The Conservative Party Commission report 'Strengthening Parliament' described this process in 2000 as 'close to preposterous'. [392] Scrutiny problems are also posed because an SI can be published after it has come into force, or it may be scheduled to come into force before the time allotted for scrutiny is complete; and often the implications of the regulations, particularly for other domestic or EU legislation

---

[392] Professor the Lord Norton of Louth (2000), *Strengthening Parliament: The Report of the Commission to Strengthen Parliament* (London: Conservative Party).

may not be immediately apparent. And a key factor favouring the executive, and hindering the willingness of some parliamentarians to spend much time on scrutiny of delegated legislation, is the fact that they cannot be amended or redrafted in any way. MPs can either accept the SI in full, or reject it.

Successive reports have recommended major reform of the process and procedures governing delegated legislation to no avail. The Rippon Commission recommended that departmental select committees should review SIs in their field prior to their being laid before Parliament and then report on any matters of particular importance. It also suggested that a Legislation Steering Committee should determine which prayers should be debated thus removing control over the allocation of time for debate from government business managers. Once an SI was selected for debate it should then be referred to a special committee that should undertake detailed scrutiny, exploring not just technical issues but also the underlying purpose, meaning and effect of the instrument.

The Procedure Committee also explored reform of the process in 1996 and 2000 but it too made little progress. Its core recommendation was the introduction of a sifting committee in both Houses to consider the political and legal significance of individual SIs, with the power to call for further information from government departments where necessary. These committees would then recommend which negative procedure instruments ought to be debated, irrespective of whether a member had 'prayed' against them, and which affirmative instruments could be agreed to without debate, unless six members demanded one.

The House of Lords adopted the sifting committee proposal in the form of the Merits of Statutory Instruments Committee three years later. But none of the committee's recommendations were implemented in the House of Commons where the government argued that a sifting committee might lead to significantly increased demands on parliamentary time.

In recent years the debate about the inadequacy of delegated legislation has powerfully re-emerged. The far-reaching powers contained in the 2006 Legislative and Regulatory Reform Bill was such that it was jocularly renamed by commentators as the 'Abolition of Parliament Bill'. [393] Much of the current

---

[393] A. Brazier, S. Kalitowski & G. Rosenblatt with M. Korris (2008), *Law in the Making: Influence and Change in the Legislative Process* (London: Hansard Society), p.115.

debate concerns the use of Henry VIII clauses that allow ministers to amend primary legislation without recourse to Parliament. The recent Public Bodies Bill 2010 illustrates the problem. The House of Lords Constitution Committee concluded that the powers in this bill 'would grant to ministers unacceptable discretion to rewrite the statute book, with inadequate parliamentary scrutiny of, and control over, the process'. [394]

So what can be done to both restrain the excessive use of executive power and improve the quality of the regulations being brought forward by the government? Firstly, in the discussions between Parliament and government to inform the development of an agreed set of criteria for legislative standards, **agreement should be sought on the criteria to be used for deciding the specific form of Statutory Instruments being utilised in any bill.** At present it is unclear how government decides which measures are to be dealt with under the negative, affirmative and super-affirmative procedures. For each bill **the government should then outline in the new Legislative Impact Assessment specifically what delegated powers are proposed in the primary legislation and why,** for consideration by the Legislative Standards Committee.

The House of Commons should establish its own sifting committee similar to the Lords Merits of Statutory Instruments Committee to complement the scrutiny work carried out by peers. It is worth noting here that both the Scottish Parliament and the Welsh Assembly have established dedicated committees to consider delegated legislation. It is unacceptable that the House of Commons has not.

Praying time on SIs should be extended from 40 to 60 sitting days in order to provide more time for consideration, and **the affirmative resolution procedure for regulations should allow for amendment not just wholesale adoption or rejection.** Debates on SIs – whether in the Chamber or in committee – could be modelled on the procedures adopted for European Committees, namely questions to the minister followed by the debate. [395]

---

[394] House of Lords Delegated Powers and Regulatory Reform Committee (2010-11), *Public Bodies Bill [HL]*, HL 57, p.3.

[395] R. Rogers & O. Gay, 'Suggestions for possible changes to the procedure and business of the House – a note by the Clerks', House of Commons Parliament and Constitution Research Centre note, SN/PC/05110, 18 June 2009, paras. C20-21, p.7.

The complexity of modern government is such that the increased use of delegated legislation is likely to continue apace in the future. SIs are highly technical and demand a high degree of intricate knowledge of areas of policy such as social welfare, the environment or health and safety regulations. Given both the volume of SIs and their level of technicality, Parliament ought to consider whether it is always the body best placed to scrutinise them. **Reform of the scrutiny processes for delegated legislation is a most urgent priority.** As part of any review of that scrutiny process, **consideration should be given to the value of extra-parliamentary scrutiny** through the establishment of a number of independent bodies, similar in form and scope to the Social Security Advisory Committee (SSAC) whose work examining delegated legislation arising from social security policy and statutes was outlined in chapter 2. In specific policy areas that generate high levels of very technical regulations, such bodies may be far better placed to comment and advise on the content of the SIs than parliamentarians. However, to assure the role of Parliament, any such independent review body should establish a clear reporting function to the relevant departmental select committee(s). The SSAC consults with and sometimes meets with the Work and Pensions Select Committee and the relationship between them has in recent years been a helpful and productive one. If extra-parliamentary scrutiny was to be adopted in a broader range of policy areas then the accountability function should be clarified and formalised on a permanent basis.

Public engagement in the legislative process

Parliament is at its strongest when it is responsive to, articulates and mobilises public opinion. It is widely accepted that the process of law-making will be better if not just technical experts play a greater role in the legislative process, but also the wider public.

The public engagement section of the Wright Committee report was disappointingly weak, reflecting the inability of members to reach a consensus on how and to what degree the public should be involved in the parliamentary process.[396] It did, however, recommend a new system for petitions, to be administered by the Procedure Committee for a trial period, and further consideration of the implementation and costing of a system of ePetitions. The

---

[396] Reform of the House of Commons Committee (2008-09), *Rebuilding the House*, HC 1117.

Hansard Society has long argued that petitions and ePetitions should be made a much more significant feature of the work of Parliament in order to better engage the public and be more responsive to matters of topical public concern. The *Audit of Political Engagement* shows that the public are much more likely to sign a petition than they are to engage in any other form of democratic activity other than voting. [397] As such, **the introduction of a petitions system would have symbolic as well as practical value in better linking Parliament and the public. It is therefore vital that the trial of a new petitions and ePetitions system through a new Petitions Committee is implemented as soon as possible and reviewed after an appropriate length of time.** It is possible, even likely, that suggestions for legislative initiatives will be made through the petitions system and clear processes need to be established to ensure that relevant petitions are brought to the attention of members when legislation which is the subject of a petition is being scrutinised in Parliament.

However, a potentially more compelling process for facilitating direct input – by experts and members of the general public – into the legislative scrutiny process will be through the coalition's proposed online 'public reading' stage for government bills. [398] This will be followed by an allotted 'public reading day' for the PBC to give consideration to the public's comments on the legislation. By necessity this process needs to be enabled through the use of digital media. Parliament therefore needs to consider a centrally hosted web-based engagement platform from which the public can review the bill and make comment in a single location, with bill texts and explanatory materials made available in a machine-readable format so that third-party websites can host discussions and so that Parliament can receive comments direct from these sites. Our research tells us that if this process is to work it must be open, transparent, well-managed (including rigorous moderation) and above all it must be clear to the public how their comments have been considered and acted on. Ensuring good quality feedback to those who participate in the process is essential good practice. [399]

---

[397] Hansard Society (2010), *Audit of Political Engagement 7* (London: Hansard Society), p.81.

[398] HM Government (2010), *The Coalition: our programme for government*, p.27.

[399] A. Williamson & L. Miller (2010), *Digital Dialogues: Guide and Toolkit* (London: Hansard Society), pp.24-26.

A concordat between Parliament and government

In order to facilitate the making of better law in the future, the reforms set out in this study will require a significant level of co-operation and commitment on the part of both Parliament and government. The drawing up of mutually agreed criteria on legislative quality standards, the establishment of a House Business Committee, a renewed commitment to pre-legislative and post-legislative scrutiny, wholesale reform of the way in which delegated legislation is considered, and reform of the House of Lords will all require a change in the way that both government and Parliament operate. Some of these changes will be administrative and procedural; but considerable attitudinal and cultural change will also be required. In short, the way in which Westminster and Whitehall interact and engage with each other must be fundamentally transformed.

Given the scale of this programme of legislative reform, set alongside the broader context of constitutional reform that has taken place over the last 13 years, **we recommend that a comprehensive review of the legislative powers of the executive and Parliament be undertaken with a view to drawing up a concordat** which clearly sets out where key powers lie, and clarifies the relationships between and responsibilities of the executive, the legislatures and the courts. The review should therefore embrace a study of the relationship between Westminster and the other legislatures in the United Kingdom, and with the courts and supra-national institutions such as the EU. Such a review was recommended – 'based on the centrality of the Westminster Parliament' – by the Conservative Commission to Strengthen Parliament in 2000. [400] Similarly, a concordat clearly setting out the significant powers of scrutiny and initiation for Parliament was recommended by the Power Inquiry in 2006. [401] In 2007, responding to the Governance of Britain green paper, the Hansard Society recommended that steps should be taken to better define the relationship between Parliament and government. And the Speaker, John Bercow, has indicated he too favours such a change: 'It is important for the House of Commons to be more formal about its own

---

[400] Professor the Lord Norton of Louth (2000), *Strengthening Parliament: The Report of the Commission to Strengthen Parliament* (London: Conservative Party).

[401] The Power Inquiry (2006), *Power to the People: The report of Power: An Independent Inquiry into Britain's Democracy* (London: The Power Inquiry), p.21.

authority and be willing to enshrine powers as it reclaims them, as it demonstrated its capacity to do with the Wright Committee reforms. If we need to codify conventions to ensure that they are respected then we should do just that.' [402]

Whilst not in any way underplaying the challenges that negotiation and adoption of such a concordat would pose, it would nonetheless be a very serious demonstration on the part of both Parliament and government that they recognise that the current way in which law is made is deficient; that they are committed to the process of reform; and that they are determined to ensure everything possible is done to assure the making of better law in the future.

---

[402] John Bercow MP, Henley Management School Lecture, '10 areas of possible reform for next Parliament', 25 March 2010.

Conclusion

There will never be a process that produces perfect laws. Legislation is a critical part of the democratic process and as such will always be subject to public, party political and media pressures. As one seminar participant described it, 'bills often clothe in legislative text what may be profound disagreement on principles, and the legislative process must provide for these to be exposed if not mediated'. That disagreement also extends to the issue of parliamentary reform itself. Parliament does not posses its own blueprint for change in part because of the lack of consensus within the institution itself about what reform means. Members rarely have an overarching vision outlining the scope and objectives of change and there are no effective mechanisms in place to facilitate implementation and then periodic review of any changes that are made.

What we have set out here is therefore a comprehensive long-term programme for reform addressing the inter-connected areas of policy development, preparation and scrutiny. If better law is to be made in the future it is essential that steps are taken to improve consultation, drafting and consideration of law within both government and Parliament.

This study shows that the issues of time and volume are inextricably linked and that enduring procedural progress will not be made unless operational reforms are accompanied by a significant change in the culture and attitude of government and parliamentarians towards the law-making process. A number of the tools that would demonstrably help improve the quality of legislation are already in existence but they are not sufficiently embedded in the day-to-day work of government and Parliament to make a significant and sustained difference.

Binding together the reform proposals set out in the preceding chapters are a number of common themes and principles.

Parliament should be less supine in the face of the government's desire to legislate – the executive has a right to implement its legislative programme but Parliament has an obligation to ensure that the laws that are passed are of the highest possible quality, having been subject to appropriate levels of consultation, preparation and scrutiny. As Leader of the House, Sir George

Young, has noted, 'the government is formed from Parliament – it doesn't own it'. [403]

The programme of procedural reforms adopted should collectively amount to a system of checks and balances to encourage the executive wherever possible, and to provide some restraint if necessary – as with the recommended adoption of a mutually agreed policy of minimum standards of legislative preparation.

Cultural and attitudinal change may pose the biggest challenge to the making of better law. Therefore 'good behaviour' in terms of an adoption of the highest possible standards of legislative consultation, preparation and deliberation should be incentivised within the procedural system. So, for example, a failure to reach mutual agreement on programming would carry the prospective penalty of an additional day's debate on the programming motion; or if the agreed legislative standards are not met then Parliament might decide to defer consideration of a bill.

There is an opportunity, through adoption of a broad approach to reform, to streamline the legislative system such that whilst there may not be time-savings to be made, it should not take longer to pass laws. Rather, more efficient and effective use of existing time could be made. Parliament should also take a more bi-cameral approach to the consideration of legislation, ensuring that the respective strengths and expertise of each House are deployed to best effect.

Government and Parliament should recognise that they do not have a monopoly on expertise, particularly in highly technical fields of law, and may not always be the people best placed to deliberate on the merits of such complex legislation. Within agreed and limited parameters some legislative proposals might be subject to more effective, forensic scrutiny by other experts. Engagement of external expertise in the drafting process, greater outreach to researchers and policy experts at the policy development and consultation stage, and provision for some extra-parliamentary scrutiny particularly of delegated legislation may all help to improve law-making in the long-term,

---

[403] Sir George Young MP, 'Parliamentary Reform: The Conservative Perspective' lecture delivered on 18 March 2010, in Hansard Society (2010), *The Reform Challenge – Perspectives on Parliament: Past, Present and Future* (London: Hansard Society), p.51.

providing that the issue of accountability to Parliament is addressed as an integral part of the reform process.

There are also, at each stage of the law-making process, lessons to be learnt by Whitehall and Westminster from other jurisdictions. For example, at the consultation stage, valuable guidance and advice might be gleaned from the co-production research models used in other parts of the world, and from the emergence of knowledge brokers and policy entrepreneurs. A number of international exemplars for writing laws in plain language could also be utilised in the Westminster context. Then, at the scrutiny stage in Parliament, performance could be enhanced by provision of more detailed supporting information about a bill in the form of a new legislative impact assessment and expanded explanatory notes, and through the piloting of a legislative scrutiny committee model – for all of which Westminster might look to the devolved legislatures in Scotland and Wales for guidance.

In approaching reform, Parliament and government should not be afraid to test, innovate, evaluate, learn and revise. They do not have the luxury of starting from a blank slate; they have to build on the organic accretion of past reforms and practices. A history of piecemeal reform exacts a price: new measures may de-stabilise the use of existing procedures and create inconsistencies and unintended consequences that undermine the coherence and rationality of the process as a whole. That is why it is important not to cherry-pick only those reforms that are perhaps most likely to attract political and popular support and coincidentally are often the easiest ones to implement. To be truly effective any reforms must be intellectually coherent and cohesive; offered as a blueprint package of interrelated proposals not a disparate group of independent options. As the limited success of the programming reform demonstrates, there are unfortunate consequences when one reform is detached from other reforms to which it was directly related and upon which its success depended, at least in part. When it is clear that a reform is not working as intended there should be mechanisms to review and reform it further if necessary; reform should be treated as an ongoing process not a one-off initiative. This will require both Parliament and government to determine internal mechanisms to facilitate an ongoing process of evaluation and review.

Finally, improving legislation is a goal that will not be accomplished cheaply for there is a cost attached to ensuring the delivery of good consultation, drafting and scrutiny processes. Establishing new mechanisms and bodies for improved oversight and scrutiny will come at a price; providing mobile IT facilities for members in the Chambers and committees to enable them to better understand the legislative proposals before them will require investment; and improving the explanatory and information materials that are provided with bills will impose a greater burden on budgets than at present. In the current economic climate in which the parties have committed themselves to 'cutting the cost of politics' it may be deemed difficult to make the necessary business case for these initiatives and reforms. However, that would be a false economy, for the introduction of deficient legislation currently carries a cost that has never been fully calculated and indeed is so complex it is perhaps incalculable. Investment in reform to improve legislation would pay dividends in the future. Greater value might also be extracted from the government's current reform plans – particularly, for example, its proposals for a Fixed Term Parliament. This reform could deliver some significant advantages in terms of improved management of time – but this will only be fully realised when accompanied by linked procedural reforms.

History suggests that the best opportunities for parliamentary and legislative reform come at the start of a new Parliament and often when there is a new government that is keen to demonstrate how different it is to its predecessors. In 1979 the incoming Conservative government introduced departmental select committees; and in 1997, the incoming Labour administration committed to a broader plan for reform encompassing, for example, programming, pre-legislative scrutiny, and sessional carry-over.

Lord Norton of Louth has argued that significant parliamentary reform demands a 'window of opportunity' and that three conditions must usually be fulfilled: a general election must recently have been held; a clear reform agenda must have been set out, providing a coherent set of proposals for MPs to unite behind; and there has to be political leadership and commitment. [404] Beyond this 'window', political zeal for change fades over the course of a Parliament and the opportunity for significant reform consequently declines. A reform agenda can also be simply overwhelmed, quite quickly, by the sheer scale of the government's legislative programme.

---

[404] P. Norton, 'Reforming Parliament in the United Kingdom', *Journal of Legislative Studies*, 6(3), 2000, pp.1-15.

The handling of the government's early bills has raised alarm bells about the extent of the coalition's commitment to legislative reform. However, in recent months the Deputy Leader of the House, Liberal Democrat MP David Heath, has reassured members that there will be a significant increase in the number of bills sent in draft to select committees for pre-legislative scrutiny [405], a position echoed by the Conservative Leader of the House of Lords, Lord Strathclyde. [406] Heath has also indicated a desire to see improvements in the use of time in the House of Commons, suggesting that if the House 'adopts a rational approach to the important things that need to be debated at length and those that may not need to be debated at quite such length, the House can start to look like a grown-up legislature able to do its job effectively'. [407] And the Conservative Leader of the House, Sir George Young, for many years a vocal advocate of parliamentary reform, has indicated a desire to engage in 'sensible discussions' to see if consensus can be achieved with the opposition about the timetabling of bills. [408]

It remains to be seen whether these commitments will be delivered. But at the start of this new Parliament the prospect of reform is a live possibility. There is a window of opportunity for substantial reform given the coalition government's commitment to a 'new politics', to a broad package of political and constitutional reforms, and their oft-repeated criticisms of the legislative process whilst in opposition. [409] We hope this study will help to initiate a political and public debate about what reforms are needed and why, if the process of law-making from policy to Act is to be improved to the benefit of all of us, in the future.

---

[405] David Heath MP, *Hansard*, 25 October 2010, vol. 517 col. 21.

[406] Lord Strathclyde, *Hansard*, 28 October 2010, vol. 721 cols. 1306-1307.

[407] David Heath MP, *Hansard*, 25 October 2010, vol. 517 col. 20.

[408] Sir George Young MP, *Hansard*, 28 October 2010, vol. 517 col. 465.

[409] See, for example, Conservative Party, *'Big Ideas To Give Britain Real Change'*, 24 April 2010, p.7.

Appendix I
List of seminar participants[410]

Seminar 1: Bad law: a diagnosis – 26 March 2009

Seminar 2: Moving from policy to law: the role of external expertise – 2 June 2009

Seminar 3: Drafting better law – 8 July 2009

Seminar 4: Innovations in legislative scrutiny – 28 October 2009

NOTE: Those who presented a paper or served as a panel discussant at one of the seminars are marked with an '*' below.

Sarah Beasley, Clerk, National Assembly for Wales

Lord Bichard, Director, Institute for Government*

Fiona Booth, Chief Executive, Hansard Society

Alex Brazier, Hansard Society Fellow

Keith Bush, Director of Legal Services, National Assembly for Wales

Professor Damian Chalmers, Professor of European Union Law, London School of Economics

Michael Clancy, Director of Law Reform, Law Society of Scotland*

Rob Clements, Director of Service Delivery, Department of Information Services, House of Commons

Christine Cogger, Legal Services Office, House of Commons

Francis Coleman, Office of the Parliamentary Counsel

Anita Coles, Policy Officer, Liberty

Emily Commander, Scrutiny Unit, House of Commons

Professor Philip Cowley, Professor of Parliamentary Government, Nottingham University*

---

[410] The job titles/positions given are as they were at the time of the seminar series.

Veronica Daly, Assistant Counsel, House of Commons

Rosemary Davies, Legal Director, Ministry of Justice

Peter Davis, Legal Services Officer, House of Commons

Guy Dehn, Director, Witness Confident

Paul Double, Remembrancer, City of London

Steven Durno, Legal Policy Officer, Law Society

Paul Evans, Principal Clerk of Select Committees, House of Commons

David Faulkner, Better Government Initiative

Sir Christopher Foster, Chairman, Better Government Initiative

Dr Ruth Fox, Hansard Society

Elizabeth Gardiner, Office of the Parliamentary Counsel

Oonagh Gay, Head of Parliament & Constitution Centre, House of Commons Library

Virginia Gibbons, Hansard Society

Michael Hallsworth, Researcher, Institute for Government

Matthew Hamlyn, Head of Unit, Scrutiny Unit, House of Commons

Baroness Hamwee*

Dr Elinor Harper, Immigration Law Practitioners' Association

Alison Harvey, Immigration Law Practitioners' Association

Adrian Hogarth, Office of the Parliamentary Counsel

Professor Jeremy Horder, Criminal Law Commissioner, Law Commission*

Helen Holden, Parliament & Constitution Centre, House of Commons Library

Chris Huhne MP*

Helen Irwin, former Clerk, House of Commons

Joanest Jackson, Senior Legal Adviser, National Assembly for Wales

Kate Jenkins, Vice-chair, Hansard Society

Richard Kelly, Parliament & Constitution Centre, House of Commons Library

Matt Korris, Hansard Society

Stephen Laws CB, First Parliamentary Counsel*

Liam Laurence Smyth, Clerk of the Journals, House of Commons

Sir Tom Legg, Better Government Initiative

Jessica Levy, Office of Tony Wright MP

Professor Martin Loughlin, Professor of Public Law, London School of Economics

Chintan Makwana, Administrative Assistant, Public Bill Office / Journal Office, House of Commons

Sir Nicholas Monck, Better Government Initiative

Marie Navarro, Research Associate, Cardiff Law School

Jan Newton OBE, former adviser, Department for Education and Schools

Professor the Lord Norton of Louth, Director of the Centre for Legislative Studies and Professor of Government, University of Hull*

Professor Dawn Oliver, Professor of Constitutional Law, University College London

Baroness O'Neill of Bengarve, Chair, Nuffield Foundation

Professor Ed Page, Sidney and Beatrice Webb Professor of Public Policy, London School of Economics

Crispin Poyser, Committee Office, House of Commons

Beverley Richardson, Office of the Parliamentary Counsel

Professor Genevra Richardson, Professor of Law, King's College London

Peter Riddell, Chair, Hansard Society

Robert Rogers, Assistant Clerk and Director of Chamber and Committee Services, House of Commons*

Dr Meg Russell, Deputy Director, Constitution Unit, University College London

Geoffrey Sellers, Office of the Parliamentary Counsel

Michael Smyth, Head of Public Policy Practice, Clifford Chance

Chris Stanton, Public Bill Office, House of Commons

Dr Diana Stirbu, Hansard Society

Jonathan Teasdale, Law Commission

Sir Richard Tilt, Chair, Social Security Advisory Committee*

Anthony Tomei, Director, Nuffield Foundation

Professor Stefan Vogenauer, Director of the Oxford Institute of European and Comparative Law and Professor of Comparative Law, Brasenose College, Oxford*

Professor Helen Wallace, Centennial Professor, European Institute London School of Economics

Gareth Williams, Clerk, National Assembly for Wales

Tania Williams, Legal Policy Team, Ministry of Justice

Sharon Witherspoon, Nuffield Foundation

Johannes M. Wolff, Better Regulation Executive, Department for Business, Innovation & Skills

Stephen Worthington QC, Law Reform Committee, Bar Council

Appendix II
Overview of the legislative process

Bills can start out life in the House of Commons or the House of Lords. The titles of bills that begin in the Lords have the suffix [HL].

First reading: the bill is published and its title is read out in the House in which it has been introduced, but there is no debate.

Second reading: the first debate a bill receives, focused on the broad principles and intentions of the bill. It is very unusual for a bill to be rejected at this stage.

Money resolutions and ways and means resolutions: any bill that involves a charge on central government funds requires approval of a money resolution, and a bill involving the levying of taxes or other charges requires a ways and means resolution. These resolutions are not debatable if they are moved immediately after second reading; otherwise, they may be debated for up to 45 minutes.

Committee: the bill is considered line-by-line by a group of MPs chosen by the party whips. Amendments are tabled, debated and voted upon. In 2007 standing committees, as they had been known, were replaced by public bill committees, which are able to take external evidence.

For particularly significant bills, finance bills or those of constitutional importance, committee stage in the Commons can take place in the main Chamber, allowing all MPs to participate. This is known as a Committee of the Whole House. In the Lords the majority of bills are considered in this manner, though some are debated outside the Chamber in Grand Committee, although no votes may take place.

Report: the bill as amended in committee is returned to the main Chamber for debate and further amendment. If the bill has been subjected to a Committee of the Whole House, report stage is skipped.

Third reading: the amended bill is considered as a whole again, and if approved it is sent to the other House. Third readings are often taken immediately after report stage, and involve only a short debate.

Consideration of amendments: if the other House amends a bill, it returns to the House in which it originated to be considered again. If the amendments are accepted, the bill goes for Royal Assent, and becomes law. If the amendments are rejected by the originating House, the bill is sent back to the second House for further consideration. Disagreements between the two Houses can lead to 'ping-pong', where the bill is sent back and forth until agreement is reached or, very rarely, the bill is abandoned.

Royal Assent: the bill is signed by the Queen, becoming an Act of Parliament and the law of the land.

Figure 1: Example of a bill originating in the Commons [411]

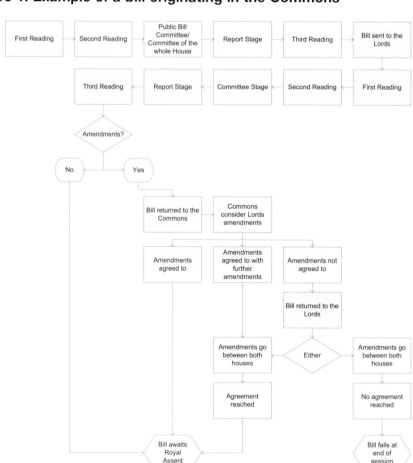

---

[411] House of Commons Information Office (June 2007), *Factsheet L1: Parliamentary Stages of a Government Bill* (London: House of Commons).

Appendix III

The legislative process in Scotland and Wales

Scottish Parliament – stages in the passage of a public bill [412]

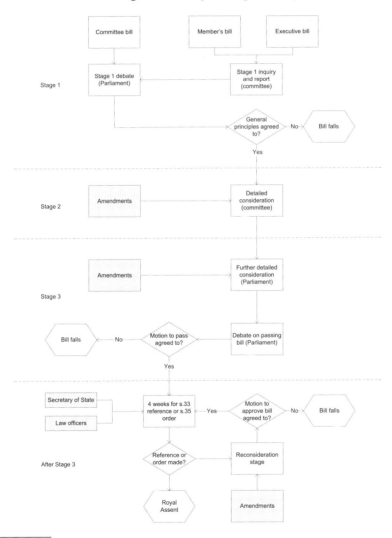

---

[412] Scottish Parliament, Guidance on Public Bills, http://www.scottish.parliament.uk/business/bills/billguidance/gpb-AnnexE.pdf.

National Assembly for Wales – stages in the passage of a Measure [413]

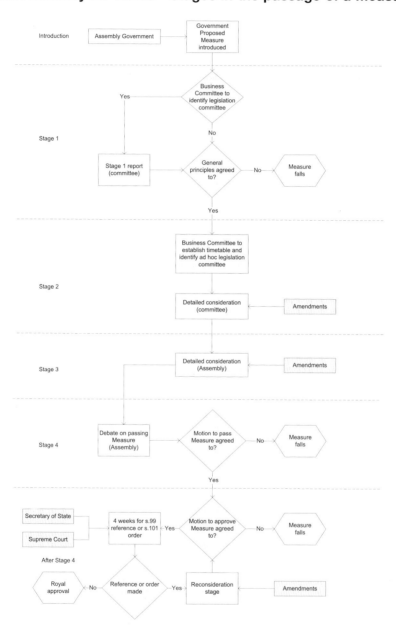

[413] National Assembly for Wales, Measures Guidance, http://www.assemblywales.org/bus-home/bus-legislation/bus-legislation-guidance/bus-legislation-guidance-measures.htm.

Appendix IV

Home Office legislation under Labour 1997-2010 [414]

- Firearms (Amendment) (No. 2) Act 1997
- Special Immigration Appeals Commission Act 1997
- Crime and Disorder Act 1998
- Criminal Justice (Terrorism and Conspiracy) Act 1998
- Nuclear Explosions (Prohibition and Inspections) Act 1998
- Football (Offences and Disorder) Act 1999
- Immigration and Asylum Act 1999
- Youth Justice and Criminal Evidence Act 1999
- Criminal Justice and Courts Services Act 2000
- Football (Disorder) Act 2000
- Race Relations (Amendment) Act 2000
- Regulation of Investigatory Powers Act 2000
- Sexual Offences (Amendment) Act 2000
- Terrorism Act 2000
- Criminal Justice and Police Act 2001
- Vehicles (Crime) Act 2001
- Anti-terrorism, Crime and Security Act 2001
- Civil Defence (Grant) Act 2002
- Criminal Defence Service (Advice and Assistance) Act 2001
- Football (Disorder) (Amendment) Act 2002
- Nationality, Immigration and Asylum Act 2002
- Police Reform Act 2002
- Proceeds of Crime Act 2002
- Anti-social Behaviour Act 2003
- Crime (International Co-operation) Act 2003
- Criminal Justice Act 2003
- Extradition Act 2003
- Sexual Offences Act 2003

---

[414] In 2007 responsibility for control of probation, prisons and prevention of re-offending was moved from the Home Office to the Department for Constitutional Affairs, which was renamed the Ministry of Justice. Legislation such as the Offender Management Act 2007, which would previously have been managed by the Home Office, was instead the responsibility of the Ministry of Justice.

- Asylum and Immigration (Treatment of Claimants, etc.) Act 2004
- Domestic Violence, Crime and Victims Act 2004
- Drugs Act 2005
- Prevention of Terrorism Act 2005
- Serious Organised Crime and Police Act 2005
- Fraud Act 2006
- Identity Cards Act 2006
- Immigration, Asylum and Nationality Act 2006
- Police and Justice Act 2006
- Racial and Religious Hatred Act 2006
- Terrorism Act 2006
- Violent Crime Reduction Act 2006
- Corporate Manslaughter and Corporate Homicide Act 2007
- Serious Crime Act 2007
- UK Borders Act 2007
- Counter-Terrorism Act 2008
- Borders, Citizenship and Immigration Act 2009
- Policing and Crime Act 2009
- Crime and Security Act 2010

Appendix V

Volume of legislation: facts and figures

The following information has been sourced from research papers published by the House of Commons Library and House of Commons Sessional Returns. [415]

Bills & Acts

Table 1: Primary legislation – Public Bills

Session	Public Bills introduced	Of which: Government bills	Public Bills receiving Royal Assent
1997-98 (7.5.97-19.11.98)	202	53	62
1998-99 (24.11.98-11.11.99)	135	31	35
1999-00 (17.11.99-30.11.00)	144	40	45
2000-01 (6.12.00-14.5.01)	89	26	21
2001-02 (13.6.01-7.1.02)	162	39	47
2002-03 (13.11.02-20.11.03)	138	36	46
2003-04 (26.11.03-18.11.04)	131	36	38
2004-05 (23.11.04-7.4.05)	88	32	21
2005-06 (11.5.05-8.11.06)	179	58	56
2006-07 (15.11.06-30.10.07)	131	34	33
2007-08 (06.11.07-26.11.08)	138	32	33
2008-09 (03.12.08-12.11.09)	138	26	27
2009-10 (18.11.09-08.04.10)	92	26	30

---

[415] R. Cracknell, *Acts & Statutory Instruments: Volume of UK legislation 1950 to 2007*, Standard Note SG/2911, January 2008,(London: House of Commons Library); S. Lightbown & B. Smith (August 2009), *Parliamentary Trends: Statistics About Parliament, Research Paper 09/69*, August 2009, (London: House of Commons Library).

Table 2: Draft Bills

Session	Draft Bills Published	Draft Bills scrutinised by a committee
1997-98	3	2
1998-99	6	5
1999-00	6	3
2000-01	2	1
2001-02	7	6
2002-03	9 *	10
2003-04	12 **	10
2004-05	5 ***	2
2005-06	4	3
2006-07	4	3
2007-08	9 ****	7
2008-09	7	3
2009-10	2	1

* includes draft clauses of the Police (Northern Ireland) Bill.

** some clauses of the draft Gambling Bill were published in Session 2002-03.

*** includes draft clauses of the Company Law Reform Bill, further clauses were published in Session 2005-06

**** includes the Immigration and Citizenship Bill, of which only part was published in draft form

Acts and Statutory Instruments

The following charts show the number of public Acts which have received Royal Assent and Statutory Instruments which have been made by UK Government departments and other UK authorities, the National Assembly for Wales (since 1999) and registered by the Statutory Instruments Registrar. For consistency it also includes statistics relating to Scottish Statutory Instruments made by the Scottish Administration since 1999 and registered by the Scottish Statutory Instruments Registrar.

Figure 2:

Acts Passed 1950-2010

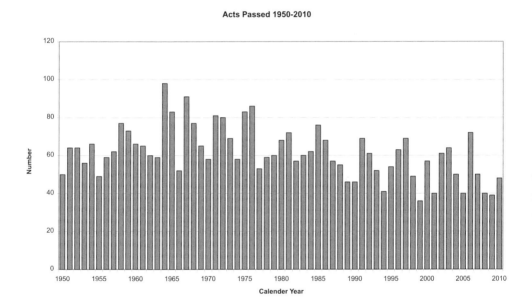

The trend in the number of acts passed is for a decline over the last 30-40 years. However the number of statutory instruments has seen a sharp increase from around 2,000 a year until the late 1980s to around double that now.

Figure 3:

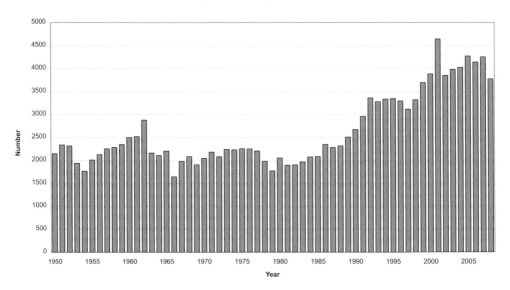

Data underpinning Figures 2 and 3 is in Table 3.

Table 3: Number of Public General Acts and Statutory Instruments 1950 to 2010 [416]

Year	Total Acts	Total SI	Year	Total Acts	Total SI
1950	50	2144	1980	68	2051
1951	64	2335	1981	72	1892
1952	64	2312	1982	57	1900
1953	56	1937	1983	60	1965
1954	66	1764	1984	62	2072
1955	49	2007	1985	76	2080
1956	59	2122	1986	68	2344
1957	62	2250	1987	57	2278
1958	77	2280	1988	55	2311
1959	73	2342	1989	46	2503
1960	66	2495	1990	46	2667
1961	65	2514	1991	69	2953
1962	60	2877	1992	61	3359
1963	59	2157	1993	52	3276
1964	98	2102	1994	41	3334
1965	83	2201	1995	54	3345
1966	52	1641	1996	63	3291
1967	91	1976	1997	69	3114
1968	77	2079	1998	49	3319
1969	65	1902	1999	36	3692
1970	58	2044	2000	57	3878
1971	81	2178	2001	40	4641
1972	80	2077	2002	61	3846
1973	69	2236	2003	64	3976
1974	58	2227	2004	50	4018
1975	83	2251	2005	40	4266
1976	86	2248	2006	72	4134
1977	53	2202	2007	50	4246
1978	59	1977	2008	40	3768
1979	60	1770	2009	39	n/a
			2010	48	n/a

[416] Excludes Northern Ireland Acts and statutory rules 2003 includes under "Consolidation Acts" one Act under the Tax Law re-write. Source: House of Commons Library and Office of Public Sector Information

Pages of Legislation

An alternative measure of the volume of legislation passed by Parliament is the number of pages of legislation. The following chart shows the number of pages of Acts and Statutory Instruments in the published Stationery Office volumes for calendar years.

While the number of Acts has been declining over the last four decades, the number of pages of Acts has tended to increase. Statutory Instruments have grown in number and in terms of the total number of pages.

Figure 4:

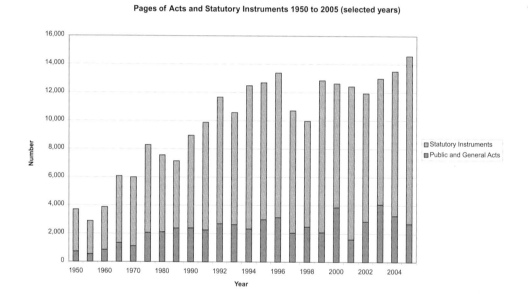

Pages of Acts and Statutory Instruments 1950 to 2005 (selected years)

Data underpinning Figure 4 is in Table 4.

Table 4: Pages of Acts and Statutory Instruments (selected years) 1911 to 2005

Year	Public and General Acts	Statutory Instruments
1911	430	330
1921	420	1,080
1931	280	1,050
1940	370	1,970
1950	720	2,970
1955	540	2,340
1960	850	3,020
1965	1,340	4,730
1970	1,110	4,880
1975	2,060	6,210
1980	2,110	5,440
1985	2,380	4,760
1990	2,390	6,550
1991	2,250	7,630
1992	2,700	8,960
1993	2,640	7,940
1994	2,340	10,140
1995	3,000	9,690
1996	3,150	10,230
1997	2,060	8,660
1998	2,490	7,480
1999	2,096	10,760
2000	3,865	8,770
2001	1,605	10,830
2002	2,868	9,070
2003	4,073	8,920
2004	3,270	10,236
2005	2,712	11,868

Notes: The figures for Statutory Instruments relate to the number of pages in the Stationery Office bound set – this excludes some local and unpublished instruments and, more recently, those of the National Assembly for Wales. The figures do not include Northern Ireland (Stormont) Acts or Statutory Rules. Pre-1987 figures are adjusted to current page sizes.

Appendix VI

Glossary

Terms related to the stages of legislation can be found in Appendix II.

Act of Parliament
A piece of legislation that has been approved by Parliament and received Royal Assent becomes law and is known as an Act.

Amendments
As a bill passes through Parliament, MPs and peers may table amendments (suggest changes) which they believe will improve the quality of the legislation. The Speaker – or the chairman in the case of standing committees – has the power to select which amendments should be debated and, if necessary, voted upon.

Annunciator
The annunciator service gives textual information about parliamentary proceedings on television screens throughout the parliamentary estate.

Backbencher
MPs and peers who do not have ministerial posts in the governing party, shadow ministerial or spokesperson roles in the opposition parties are known as backbenchers. They sit on the benches behind (or to the side) of their ministerial colleagues in Parliament.

Bills
A proposal for a new law is known as a bill once it has been introduced into Parliament at first reading. If it is approved by Parliament and has receives Royal Assent it becomes an Act.

Carry-over
Bills that do not complete their passage through Parliament in one session can, if the appropriate motion is approved, be carried over into the next session. This may not be done more than once for any single bill, and not at all for bills that started in the House of Lords.

Chairmen's Panel

The Chairmen's Panel is made up of at least 10 Members of Parliament who are nominated by the Speaker at the start of every session to act as chairmen of the five standing committees and to chair sessions in Westminster Hall.

Clauses

Every bill is made up of a number of clauses containing the provisions of the proposed legislation. Clauses are debated in numerical order during standing committee and report stages, along with selected amendments relating to it.

Command Paper

An official government publication.

Committee of Selection

The Committee of Selection is responsible for appointing members to committees. It is party whip dominated and consists of nine members.

Consolidation bill

These bills bring together a number of Acts that deal with the same subject into a single Act of Parliament. It will not, as a rule, seek to change significantly the policy represented by the original pieces of legislation.

Crossbenches

In the House of Lords several rows of benches, known as crossbenches, separating the main government and opposition frontbenches, are situated in the middle of the chamber. Lords who are not representatives of any particular political party, or who do not, for any reason, take the party whip, sit on the crossbenches of the House and are referred to as crossbenchers. Bishops and archbishops in the Lords do not sit on the crossbenches but are also non-party affiliated.

Delegated legislation

Delegated legislation is law made by ministers under powers deriving from Acts of Parliament. Thousands of pieces of delegated legislation, commonly known as Statutory Instruments, are passed by Parliament each year. They enable minor changes to the law to be made without having to introduce a whole new Act of Parliament, but which are subject to varying degrees of parliamentary scrutiny.

Divisions

A vote in Parliament is known as a division.

Early Day Motion

Early Day Motions (EDMs) are formal motions submitted for debate in the House of Commons. However, very few EDMs are actually debated. Instead, they are used for reasons such as publicising the views of individual MPs, drawing attention to specific events or campaigns, and demonstrating the extent of parliamentary support for a particular cause or point of view.

Frontbench

In the Commons, the two sets of green benches facing each other directly in front of the Speaker and the table of the house are known as the frontbenches. The government frontbench, also known as the Treasury benches, is occupied by leading members of the governing party: the Cabinet and other departmental ministers. Similarly, the shadow cabinet will occupy the opposition frontbench.

Green paper

A green paper is a consultation document issued by the government which contains policy proposals for debate and discussion before a final decision is taken on the best policy option. A green paper will often contain several alternative policy options. Following this consultation the government will normally publish firmer recommendations in a white paper.

Hansard

The name for the full transcript of proceedings of both Houses of Parliament. Also known as the Official Record. Not to be confused with the Hansard Society.

Joint committee

A committee that consists of members of both the House of Commons and the House of Lords.

Keeling Schedule

A schedule of a bill that contains a copy of a previous Act that the bill amends significantly. The Keeling Schedule shows where the provisions in the bill propose to change the original Act.

Leader of the House of Commons

The member of the government who is chiefly responsible for the arrangement of government business in the House of Commons.

Long title

This provides a description of the purposes or scope of an Act of Parliament. The long title is important as under the procedures of Parliament, a bill cannot be amended to go outside the scope of its long title. For that reason, the long title tends to be vague.

Motion
A motion is a proposal for a debate or a decision which may be voted upon if contested.

Parliamentary Counsel
Parliamentary Counsel are specialist lawyers who draft the text of bills.

Particularism
Particularism is the tendency to set out the provisions of an Act in great detail, seeking to include provisions for every possible eventuality.

Petitions
MPs may present petitions on behalf of their constituents on any topic in the main Chamber. They are of little value as they are not debated.

Post-legislative scrutiny
Assessment of the implementation and operation of legislation after it has been approved by Parliament. The government department responsible for an Act will publish a memorandum on its implementation three to five years after Royal Assent for a select committee to scrutinise.

Pre-legislative scrutiny
Involves a general inquiry or more recently the issuing of a draft bill to be considered by a parliamentary committee. It includes scrutiny of consultative documents, green papers and white papers.

Programme motion
Programme motions are used in the House of Commons to set the timetable for scrutiny of a bill.

Public bill committee
A cross-party committee in the Commons appointed to carry out line-by-line scrutiny of a specific bill. Each public bill committee is named after the bill it considers. For example, a committee considering a bill titled the Climate Bill would be called the Climate Bill Committee.

Parliamentary Business and Legislation Committee
A cabinet committee, chaired by the Leader of the House of Commons, that decides which bills will be included in the government's programme for the next

parliamentary session. The bills approved by the committee are then prepared for introduction. Formerly known as the Legislation Committee.

Purpose clause

An optional clause at the beginning of a piece of primary legislation that sets out its intended purpose.

Queen's Speech

The formal opening of Parliament is made by the Queen, who reads out the government's legislative agenda for the coming session.

Royal Assent

The assent of the monarch to a bill which has been passed by both Houses of Parliament, after which it becomes law. The monarch has not withheld the Royal Assent from a bill that has been passed by Parliament since the 18th century.

Select committees

In the House of Commons select committees examine the expenditure, administration and policy of each of the main government departments and associated public bodies. Select committees have the power to take evidence and issue reports. They are made up of MPs from across the parties, the numbers of which are reflective of their party's representation in the Commons. In the House of Lords, select committees do not mirror government departments but cover broader issues such as science and technology, the economy, the constitution and the European Union.

Speaker

The Speaker presides over the House of Commons and is responsible for keeping order during debates and ensuring that the rules of the House are obeyed. The Speaker must always act impartially and protect the right of all MPs to speak during debates.

Split committal

This involves debating some sections of a bill (usually the controversial ones) in the main Chamber of the Commons or Lords for committee stage, while the remaining less controversial or more technical clauses are debated in committee.

Standing orders

The standing orders of Parliament are the rules under which Parliament conducts its business. They regulate the way MPs behave in the Commons and the way debates are organised.

Sunset clause

A provision in a bill that gives it an 'expiry date' once it is passed into law. Sunset clauses are usually included in legislation when it is felt that Parliament should have the chance to reconsider its merits after a fixed period.

Usual channels

The usual channels is the term used to describe the relationship between the whips' offices of the government and the opposition parties.

Whips

Whips are MPs or peers appointed by each party to maintain party discipline. Part of their role is to encourage members of their party to vote in the way that their party would like in important divisions.

White paper

A white paper is a document issued by a government department which contains detailed proposals for legislation. It is the final stage before the government introduces its proposals to Parliament in the form of a bill.